Haunted

Galveston

by Amy Matsumoto

ISBN
0-9846458-9-6 (10 digit)
978-0-9846458-9-3 (13 digit)

Library of Congress Catalog Number: 2013944787

First Edition

Printed in the United States of America
Published by 23 House Publishing
SAN 299-8084
www.23house.com

This book is dedicated with love to my family – Penny, Larry, John and Wynonah Murdock, and to my husband, Jason Matsumoto.

Acknowledgements

I would like to express my sincerest thanks to the dedicated archivists at the Galveston and Texas History Center, Carol Wood and Casey E. Greene, to the Galveston Historical Foundation, Dash Beardsley, Scottie Ketner, Shannon Rowan at The Islander Magazine, 23 House Publishing, and to the resilient community of Galveston, Texas, both past and present.

Table of Contents

Confederate attack on the Forty-Third Massachusetts Volunteers at
Galveston during the Civil War (courtesy Library of Congress)

Preface

You may not believe certain parts of the stories contained
in this book... Galveston's history and ghost lore are simply
that compelling. My research was made possible because of the
generous folks at the Galveston and Texas History Center at
the Rosenberg Library in Galveston. Their extensive,
impressive, and meticulously organized archives could stand
with the best in the world. What follows is the product of
countless hours of research and interview.

When I first arrived in Galveston, I was immediately
drawn in – like a seashell grabbed by the tide and swallowed
into something already developed – but the fact that Galveston
is a small island located on the southeastern coast of Texas and
is surrounded completely by the brown, warm waters of the
Gulf only partially accounts for this existential sense of being

absorbed by the ocean. Intangible at first, this feeling; certainly the giant, rambling Victorian architecture pervading the Island, along with the above ground cemetery reminders of the nation's worst natural disaster (the Great Storm of 1900) were interest-piquing, so vastly different from its metallic neighbor Houston – that sprawling, incongruent monster – but there was something sad about the Island too, something faraway and forgotten.

The fact is that Galveston is a real, live ghost town.

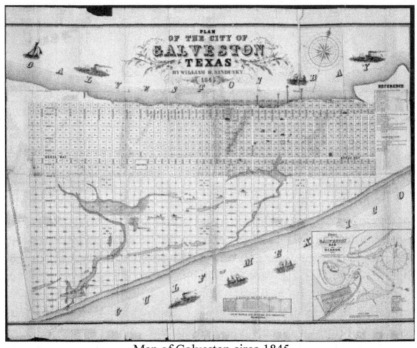

Map of Galveston circa 1845
(courtesy of Special Collections, University of Houston Libraries)

Prior to the Great Storm of 1900, the city bustled with wealth and promise. The giant rambling Victorian homes remain like symbols of that potential – like tombstones –

2

lamenting a life not fully realized. You drive over the causeway and enter another world. These beautiful homes – these once beautiful homes – are largely falling apart, left to decay and falter under the obliterating Texas sun. The Island sits like an abandoned movie set, buildings like props standing at attention, ready for someone to call "action." There are, of course, exceptions. The Galveston Historical Foundation hosts a tour every year for the public to get a first-hand look at the renovated jewels. People come from all parts of the country and world to play voyeur.

Death has defined the Island. Horrific, costly, spiraling and surprising Death. Yellow Fever. The Civil War. Ravaging fires. Hurricanes. Tragic and unexpected. Death and death and more death. Yet Galveston is not a household name like other ghost towns such as New Orleans, a fact which makes the Island's extreme paranormal context that much more unique. Perhaps more than any other American city, Galveston is both literally and figuratively haunted by its past – the devastation of events rattle like chains in the attic – a constant, steady, and invisible force beyond which life struggles. Downstairs Galveston sits, listening to their ghosts with a curious and at times ambivalent acceptance.

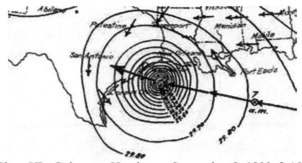

Chart XL, Galveston Hurricane, September 8, 1900, 8 AM
(courtesy National Oceanic and Atmospheric Administration)

The 1900 Storm Letters

History was made on Galveston Island on September 8, 1900. Isaac Cline, Chief of the U.S. Weather Service Bureau in Galveston described the onset of the country's worst natural disaster as a "beautiful day." Cline would later watch helplessly as his children struggled to stay afloat amid a blackened, flooded night, his pregnant wife gasping her final breath before vanishing underneath the dank, murderous waters forever. The infamous hurricane, stealing thousands of lives, left more carnage in its wake than any American storm before or since. Galveston's historic and well-toured above-ground cemeteries remain like gothic centerpieces, the giant engraved markers monstrous, like stone symbols of a tragedy never to be completely overcome, a people taken before their time – a disintegrating threshold marking not a century, but one day, when the unforgiving hands of death extinguished a much coveted flame.

Letters began to pour out of town from the survivors to their loved ones around the country, giving assurances, but also describing the horrors of the storm that has come to define the City of Galveston. Today, many of the letters are displayed in

5

the Galveston and Texas History Center's 1900 Storm exhibit at Rosenberg Library in Galveston. Several of those letters have been transcribed here to illustrate the absolute destruction of the storm.

* * * * *

The following letter was written by 1900 Storm survivor to her future husband Boyer Gonzales in New York, relating her Storm experiences, including wishing to "leave Galveston forever." (Transcribed from original manuscript, as part of the Galveston and Texas History Center's 1900 Storm exhibit at Rosenberg Library in Galveston).

Monday Sept. 17, 1900

My Dear Mr. Gonzalez,

B has just handed me your letter and we all appreciate it so much. How thankful you should be that you were so many miles away from here on that memorable 8th day of September. I would be impossible for anyone to describe the horrors of that whole thing as they really were. To read the papers telling of it is like hearing children's prattle in the comparison to the reality – I guess those away from here, who have been in suspense have rally suffered more than the other who were here to experience it all, for everyone here seems stunned, and you never see any emotion displayed of any kind. Everyone is perfectly calm! We all seem to have gone through so much that we seem beyond tears. At noon when I saw people being brought in from the beach I became very much frightened and excited and begged them all to leave this house and go to Mrs. Gresham's as the wind was coming from the Northeast and this house was rocking so terribly, but Mamma and Bess wouldn't listen to me. The Bowens have been renting the Campbell house for the summer, so about 5 p.m. Mr. B came over and told us we were in danger as part of the roof was gone. We went out into the water which was to our waists but couldn't go against the wind, then to Mrs. Gresham's, so thinking of course that the Campbell house was safer than ours, we went there. That same calm which is prevailing over the whole town took possession of me then and I was able to be of great assistance to the men in keeping the door from coming in. the whole roof came in on us, and 16 of us were huddled in the vestibules and I think we could not have withstood it a half an hour longer, for when the front doors gave way we knew we should only go out to be drowned, as twas moonlight and we could see how high the water was. We fully realized our danger and stayed as closely together as possible, so if we perished we would all four go. After the water receded we went to Mrs. Lafitte, which was damaged very slightly and there we stayed for two nights, as this house is just not habitable when it rains. But Mr. Gonzalez – I had so fully made up our minds that if we were going to die that night that it was the longest time before I could fully realize that the storm was over and we were all safe! But the whole town is a perfect wreck. You can't picture the awfulness of it all. As for the dead bodies we couldn't sit on the galleries at all without seeing wagonloads of them going by. At first, people didn't realize there would be so many, and they were carried by one at a time on hilters (?), but later they had to be carted away like so much debris. There were two wagon-fulls taken from the wreck right here in front of us on the esplanade and the poor things had stiffened in the positions in which they died. Most of them with their hands clasped high in the air, in the attitude of players. The ones I saw will haunt me to my dying day! Louise and I are begging Bess to go away from here to live, and I would gladly turn my back on Galveston forever! But of course we haven't made plans as of

7

yet. Alcie came to hunt us up the day after the storm, and drops in every once in awhile to check us all, although he is one of the busiest men in our town. He said he would probably come here and stay until your house could be fixed. He is now staying with Mrs. Brown. Well I think I had better wind up this gruesome letter. I only wish I could have written a more cheerful account. We have all been sick I think from the terrible odor, and living on canned goods and brackish water, but we are all right now. If I was selfish I would wish you were here to make us all feel better, but for your own sake I advise you not to come home if you can possible help it. We all send our love to you and hope you will write soon.

Nell

Illustration of the Galveston Hurricane Storm Surge 1900
(courtesy Library of Congress)

Men carrying bodies on stretcher, surrounded by wreckage of the hurricane and flood (courtesy Library of Congress)

The following letter was written by storm survivor John D. Blagden to family in Duluth, Minnesota. Blagden was serving temporary assignment with Galveston Weather Bureau. (Transcribed from original manuscript, as part of the Galveston and Texas History Center's 1900 Storm exhibit at Rosenberg Library in Galveston).

Weather Bureau
Galveston, TX
September (?) 1900

To All at Home,
Very probably you expect to get a letter from me from here but here I am alive and without a scratch. That is what few can say in this storm swept city.

9

I have been here two weeks, to take the place of a man who is on a three months leave, after which I go back to Memphis.

Of course you have heard of the storm that passed over this place last Friday night, but you cannot realize what it really was. I have seen many severe storms but never one like this.

I remained in the office all night. It was in a building that stood the storm better than any other in the town. Though it was badly damaged and rocked frightfully in some of the blasts. In the quarter of the city where I lodged (south quart) everything was swept and nearly all drowned. The family with whom I roomed were all lost. I lost everything I brought with me from Memphis and a little money but I think eight dollars will cover my entire loss. I am among the fortunate ones.

The local forecast official, Dr. Clive lives in the same part of the city and his brother (one of the observers here) boarded with him. They did not fare so well and this house went with the rest and were out in the wreckage nearly all night. The L(?) lost his wife but after being nearly drowned themselves they save the three children. As soon as possible the next morning after the waters went down I went out to the south end to see how faired out there. I had to go through the wreckage of buildings nearly the entire distance (one mile), and when I got there I found everything swept clean. Part of it was still under water.

I could not even find the place where I had been staying. Those who had not known would not believe that that had been a part of the city. Twenty four hours before I could not help seeing bodies though I was not desirous of seeing them. I at once gave up the family with whom I stopped as lost which was proved as then their bodies have all been found. I soon got sick of the sights out there and soon returned to the office. To put things in order as best I could. When I got back to the office I found a note from the younger Clive telling me of the safety of all except the doctor's wife. They were all badly bruised from falling and drifting timber and one of the children was badly hurt and they have some fear as to her recovery.

Mr. Brom (?) our printer live in another part of the town that suffered as badly is still missing and we have given him up as lost. There is not a building in town that is not uninjured. Hundreds are living day and night cleaning away the debris and recovering the dead. It is awful every few moment a wagon full of corpses passes by our street.

The more fortunate are doing all they can to aid the sufferers, but it is impossible to care for all. There is not enough room in the buildings stills standing to shelter them all and hundreds spent the night on the street. One meets people of all degrees of destitution. People but partially clothes are the rule and are fully clothed the exception.

The city is under military rule and the streets are patrolled by armed guards.

They are expected to shoot at once anyone pilfering. I understand four have been shot today for robbing the dead.

I don't know how true they are, for that kind of rumors are different and many of them are false.

We have neither light, fuel, or water. I have gone back to candles. I am now writing by candlelight.

A famine is feared as nearly all the provisions were ruined from the water which stood from eight to fifteen feet in the streets and all communication on the island is cut off.

For me I have no fear, sleep in the office, and have food to last for some time, and water, and some means of getting more when it rains, as it frequently does here. I have made some friends here who will not let me starve.

We had warning of the storm and many saved themselves by seeking safety before the storm reached here. We were busy all day Thursday answering phone calls about it and advising

11

people to prepare for danger. But the storm was more severe than we expected.

Dr. Clive placed confidence in the strength of the home. Many went to his house for safety as it was the strongest built of any in that part of town. But of the forty odd who took refuge there less than twenty are now living.

I have been very busy since the storm and have had little sleep but I intend to make up for sleep tonight. I don't know how or where I can send this first chance.

Write soon.

Yours Truly,
John D. Blagden

Three young men inside ruins of St. Patrick's Church
(courtesy Library of Congress)

St. Lucas Terrace, under ruins 80 bodies were found after this photograph was made (courtesy Library of Congress)

The following account was written by an 8-year-old survivor Sarah Helen Littlejohn in October 1900, entitled "My Experiences in the GALVESTON STORM September 8, 1900." (Transcribed from original manuscript, as part of the Galveston and Texas History Center's 1900 Storm exhibit at Rosenberg Library in Galveston).

Saturday morning September 8, 1900. It was raining hard. My father had gone downtown and my little friend who lived who lived not far from us came over to see me before it started raining. Her name is Minnie Lee Borden.

Minnie, my two sisters and I went upstairs to play dolls. After we had been up there a few minutes my oldest sister went downstairs and came up again and said that papa had come.

Then we all went downstairs and heard papa say that the pagoda (a place where people bathe) was washed away. It was almost 12 o'clock then and it was raining hard. Papa said that the L. (?) Streetcar could ran no farther than 14th street. Papa said the weather bureau man told him so. The water was not in our yard but it was coming in about a block from our house. Minnie's father come over and took her home to her house. Mr. Borden's skylight flew off and papa went over to his house to put it on again. But in a few minutes we saw another skylight floating off. Then we could not find out if it was our or our next door, Mr. Kirkland. We at last discovered it was Mr. Kirk's.

The water was up to Papa's knees. We had some pretty jack bean vines growing up to the second story. Papa had to tear them all down.

Toward evening we looked out our front door and saw an old man going home in a wagon. He lived down the island. The water rose higher and higher and was about up to Papa's waist. About 6 o'clock we all went down into the drawing room and just then Momma raised up the window and we saw that same old man standing up to this waist in water. We could not understand him.

Momma told him to come inside out of all the rain. It seemed to me that he could not understand us for it took Momma a long time to get him to come inside. Papa at last found that he was the father of one of the school boys that went to Papa's school. I could not understand a word he said. He said he did not mind the water, but it was wind he did not like. He was an old fisherman.

The house was leaking a little bit in several places where the sliding doors are. Papa then went upstairs and came down again and told us to go upstairs. Well we all went upstairs it was getting dark and water was in the house so we had to go upstairs. First we went into one of the northwest rooms and stayed a little while then it began leaking and Papa thought of

14

the bathrooms. Of course we could not sleep on the beds. We children managed to grab up some of the pillows from the wet beds.

We had a lantern and a few of the lamps which were upstairs. The old man would not come upstairs but stayed downstairs sitting in a rocking chair with his feet against the front door. About eight or nine o'clock the clocks stopped and at that time the storm was worst – the front door blew open and the wind blew the old man across the hall.

Then Papa and the old man shut it again but it blew open again. I will tell you now what happened. Papa said he would nail down the front door but he did not have any nails. At last he took two pieces a part of shelves which were in the bathroom. Momma stood on the tub and looked out the window. My brother Harry sat on a little box.

Harry was leaning against the wall. My youngest sister Lisa sat on a little chair was leaning with her head bent over on her pillow. Papa sat on the rugs which were on the bathtub. My oldest sister Lisa (?) and I sat upon a basket.

The ceilings were leaking badly and the water felt so cold. We all were wet because the water was dripping down on us. The sounds we heard that night were just dreadful and the pipes sounded in a horrible way. About eight or nine o'clock when the wind was just roaring we heard someone crying and the next day we found a dead body right in front of our house. There were two of them a negro man and a white girl.

When Papa was going out of the bathroom to nail up the front door there was such a draught came into the bathroom that it blew out the bathroom window which Momma was standing right at it we didn't know it would go so quickly but when Papa opened the door Momma said "there goes the window pane" and it went as quickly as lightning almost.

After Papa had nailed down the front door he came in the bathroom and stayed with us. And then he went downstairs for

15

a minute and came up and said the water was going down and we could come downstairs. The water was about up to my knees and the slime and mud was plentiful. We went into the dining room and Mamma said she saw something white. We saw it was a white cottage that had drifted there during the night to the side of our house. Papa fixed the dining room table so we could sleep on it. My two sisters went to sleep but I could not sleep because a toothache and the wind kept me awake. The water was eight inches in our house.

The water went down very rapidly and at noon it was daylight Sunday morning. We looked out of the window and of all the beautiful homes that were between our home and the beach there was none left. It is just a clean sweep nothing but desolation. I can hardly realize what has happened but when I look at Gulf I knew we could not see it before the storm and it seems so strange.

The slate blew off our house but the house stood very well all for that, for Sunday morning we started to go to Mamma's sister's house two miles from ours. We did not have any water to drink and of course we got very thirsty that hot day.

Well we got started and we had to climbed over piles and piles of debris and you know we saw dead bodies and carcasses along the way and the sights were awful.

There was old poisonous mud and slime. It rained hard that morning and we got very wet. At last we got there and Mamma said we had better stay all night.

Well we stayed all night at Aunt (?) and went back again Monday evening. We stayed at Auntie's until Friday then we went away. We went to Omen(?), Texas where we stayed until October 19. Then we came home again. School opened Oct. 22. School ought to have started October the first, but the school ought to have been repaired.

The city looks more respectable than it did the day after the storm. There isn't a trace of the bathhouse left on the beach. It is nothing but a sandbank.

I don't know if we can get away or if we can out of Galveston at all. Papa has to teach school and we have to be here with him. It looks like Galveston could not be visited twice by a storm. I hope it will never happen again.

Looking North from Ursuline Academy, showing wrecked black high school building (courtesy Library of Congress)

17

A house twisted from the hurricane (courtesy Library of Congress)

The following is a letter from J.H. Hawley to his wife and child, relating his storm experience. (Transcribed from original manuscript, as part of the Galveston and Texas History Center's 1900 Storm exhibit at Rosenberg Library in Galveston))

Galveston, Tx
Sept. 18, 1900

My dear wife and daughters –

18

This the first time in the rush of business and other duties which have fallen to my lot, in which I could calmly sit down and write you of the events which have transpired since Sept. 8th. Our office desks and furniture of every description, papers, etc. are a total wreck and I have had so many thousand things to do and so many people to talk to that I could not do more than wire you from time to time. Do not think it strange of me that I have not written but I have not had a typewriter in the office and the time required for such a letter. I have sent you copies of the Daily News and the Houston Post daily and have arranged with the Galveston News to send you a copy of the paper for a month, so you may keep posted of current events. It was evident from your telegrams to me that the mere statement that I was safe and well was not sufficient and I will therefore endeavor to give you some details that will be of some interest.

I was apprised very early on the day of the 8th, of the likelihood of the great storm which swept over the city, beginning about 3 o'clock, and ending about 12 o'clock at night, and took early precautions to protect the property of ours, and such other property under my charge. I had, of course, no idea the extent to which it would come. Water in this office was four feet high, in fact, over all the counters, overthrowing all the desks and other furniture, mixing it up in an inextricable mess of confusion. The wharf front from one end of it was crushed, carrying down with it valuable goods, and in many cases, valuable lives. Fully 5000 people lost their lives and fully 3000 more suffer from injuries from slight to serious wounds.

The whole territory from 9th St. east out to the beach, and then for a distance of four and one half blocks of the densely populated district, clear out to Wellen's Lake and beyond the Harris' house has been swept away, and fully two-thirds of the inhabitants given up to the angry waves.

19

It is impossible at this time to enumerate single instances, but I cannot refrain from mentioning Mrs. Waklen, whom you no doubt remember. Early on Monday morning, when going through the long row of bodies in the morgue I lifted the pall, and found beneath it, and found with a faint smile on her lips, Mrs. Waklen, with her gray hair all matted and streaming in disordered confusion about her shoulders. I next lifted the pall of Walter Fisher, the husband of Lillie Harris, and then came to Richard Swain, who no doubt you remember, but these are simply nothing compared to the great name of people who lost their lives. I superintended the handling of bodies over the wharves at Galveston onto the barges, whence they were taken out to sea, with weights attached to them and sunk, as the only means by which they could be disposed of; at different points along the wreckage funeral pyres were erected 10 to 16 bodies piled thereon, saturated with oil, and turned, while hundreds of bodies were burned in individual instances. By Monday it was ascertained it was utterly impossible to dispense of the bodies by giving them up to the sea or by cremation.

Lillie Harris Fisher and all her children are dead; also Rebecca Harris and three of the Davenport children – but one of the Davenport children being save. Davenport, with a voice steady with the strength of a man told me all the details, and simply laid his hand in mine and said – "Mr. Hawley, we know you mourn with me. I am grateful to God for the saving of our little daughter."

Every man here has nerve and has tried to do his duty – the measure of it was that which he could do. For two days and two nights we stayed up, not knowing even that even we were tired, until we could go no further. Instances of courage and heroism are thick, for every man to have the courage necessary to meet such an occasion.

Harry and Sarah and the baby passed a most dreadful night, with flying timbers, etc,, bombarding the house in which they were, but they survived, and when they were at my house looking for me, I was at their house looking for them, and the baby, when I got there, was sleeping peacefully, although, as the servant said, he was hungry. Harry and Sarah and the baby went on board the S.S. (?) Wednesday evening and remained there until Friday, when the ship left here for New Orleans. It is Harry's intention, as soon as he has arranged for Sarah and the baby, to return at once to his duties in Galveston. It will be a great disappointment if he fails to do so.

The storm has left the city without drainage, and the limited supply of water prevents us from giving much attention, at present, to our sanitary condition. The wreckage I have referred to is fully 100 feet deep, and in many places 25 feet high, undoubtedly underneath which there still remains a great number of bodies yet to be found. Of course you understand the accumulation of filth, etc., the stench from arising from the lack of drainage from perhaps 40,000 people, must produce sanitary conditions injurious to the health to the last degree. The weather is intensely hot from the 8th of Sept. to the present time. The weather has been perfectly clear and with the sun beating down on it, odors arise making it most unbearable. There is no place in our country that is not a more desirable locality than Galveston, for the weak and helpless. I cannot invoke too strongly your remaining away from Galveston for a time, until we have gotten the city in a condition to receive healthy people. We will do all that human hands can do. 2000 men are employed daily in cleaning up, but this will not be accomplished in less than 4 or 5 weeks of constant work. We are gradually coming up out of the disaster which settled over the city, and we know that with our commercial importance we will build a city here with modern lines which will attract a citizenship from all parts of the world.

Bradley is here, working hard with his full faculties, encouraging and doing great work and good, as everybody has abiding confidence in him.

One of the saddest deaths was that of Stanley D. Spencer. He was compelled by the rising waters to seek refuge and was unable to reach his home. I heard, two days afterwards, the lowering of the body of S.D. Spencer being in the ruins and being brought to the morgue. We found his face unmarked by violence although the back part of his head was crushed in.

I will not prolong this letter any further. Give my love to all, and believe me over and always, you

Husband and father,
J.H. Hawley

A wagon hauling the bodies of the dead from the
hurricane (courtesy Library of Congress)

Sacred Heart Church in Galveston after the storm
(courtesy Library of Congress)

The following is a personal letter from a man to his mother regarding his experiences in the storm. (Transcribed from original manuscript, as part of the Galveston and Texas History Center's 1900 Storm exhibit at Rosenberg Library in Galveston)

San Antonio, TX. Sept. 14th, 1900

My Dear Mother,
I know you are anxious to hear from me. Lester (?) had already telegraphed you before I got home which I fully expected never to do. I was called to Galveston by our

23

Chapman (?) and got there Thursday morning. Everything was beautiful there then. Then Friday evening I went over to the beach and took a bath in the surf by moonlight. Quite a large number of people were there. The extremely heavy swell of the Gulf rather startled me so I did not stay in long. Saturday morning the sky looked very dark with a slight rain falling. Wind about 10 miles an hour. About 11 o'clock I heard that the breakers in the Gulf were wrecking the buildings on the shore. It was raining quicker as of then. I took a car, went down to the beach as I wanted to see how the Gulf looked in a storm. When we reached the (?) that runs out into the water – you know where that is – we could go no further as the waves had partially wrecked it. The sight was grand at that time. I watched the waves wash out and break all those shell houses. I started to go back but found all the street cars had stopped running. This was about 1230 p.m. The water had then got so high I had to walk in water above my knee with a driving rain that felt like hail when it struck my face. I was just one house getting to the hotel. I got my driver and started out again, as I was already wet so it did not make much difference. I went down to the bayside and watched the storm until 4 o'clock. The storm was gradually increasing in fury. The rain was terrible and wind blowing a gale and bringing the waters of the bay over the streets. I stayed there until the water came over the sidewalk. Then I became nervous, but never thought of what was to follow.

I walked over Tremont St. – or rather waded over as rowboats were being used then in the streets to the Tremont Hotel. I was becoming more worried by each minute. As darkness came on the terror increased. I could not leave the hotel as it was unforeseeable to live in that wind and water. The water rose about 2 ½ feet an hour until it stood 3 ½ on the floor of the hotel. You know how high that is from street level – it was 7 feet in the street.

24

I do not know how we survived that terrible night. The howl of the wind would be followed by the crashing of buildings. Each minute part of the hotel would give away and crash in. it was the most horrible experience. We were expecting each minute to be our last. The sea ran as high in the streets of the town as it did in the Gulf. The wind blew from 120 to 130 miles an hour. There were two thousand in the hotel that night. If it had gone you can guess the rest. One hour more of that wind would have killed everyone on that Island.

We all thanked God in the morning that we were permitted to see daylight again. Sunday morning I was afraid to move. When I did muster the courage to leave you cannot guess what a sight met my gaze. Newspaper cannot describe half and have only given a partial description of the calamity. The Gulf side of the Island was swept clean for six blocks from end to end of the Island. You could not believe that there had ever been a building there. The bay side was nearly in the same condition, piled high with the wreckage of boats of all kinds. Dead bodies were everywhere to be seen in all shapes. Nearly all nude as the wind and water had stripped every piece of clothing off of them. I had nothing to eat from Saturday noon until Sunday night, not even a drink of water.

The full extent of deaths will never be known. It is at least 10,000 if not more. The stench from dead bodies was terrible Sunday morning but got worse as each day's hot sun found them.

I could not get away from there or get any word out of the Island as all wires were ruined and all railroad bridges were gone, and only three boats left. The distance to the mainland was 2 ½ miles so could not swim out there. Tuesday at 4 o'clock the telegraph co. got a boat to take their men to Virginia Point – that is what the railroads use to cross the bridge. We found hundreds of cert. floating in the bay. When we got to the mainland we were happy. There were no railroads nearer than seven miles as everything had been washed away.

We all started in and walked part of the time in water up to our waist. But we were happy to be alive. After walking over the prairie- over dead animal and human bodies, we at last reached a relief train that had been sent down as far as it could get from Houston. When we saw smoke from the engine five miles distant everyone in the party yelled as loud as they could for joy.

When we reached Houston at night then reached San Antonio. I have not been able to anything since my experience in Galveston. Every little noise startles me. My nerves are gone. We will work again Monday, Sept. 17th. I wish you would come down. We have a fine little house here. I was soaked in salt water for three days. There are some good people killed in Galveston.

I never expected to see any of you again but I am still on Earth.

I am as ever your loving son,
W. W. Davis

Karankawa Indians clashing with European explorers
(courtesy Library of Congress)

The Karankawa Indians:
Galveston's Savage Beginnings

Darkness falls on the island with the stillness and intensity of a half-closed door. You walk passed the immovable darkness sensing a presence, but without the capacity to see, you keep going... increasingly anxious to get to the other side. The Strand behaves like the death of light from a snuffed candle, the immediacy of dance of day to nighttime nothingness like an unearthly possession.

Tourists scamper back to their cars and vanish with the sun, yet with the oncoming night comes also a new sort of tourist – the type of person enchanted by stories of hauntings, and ghosts banging the night away in one of the old buildings… some of which have survived magnificent storms, scathing fires, and have stood empty for decades.

According to Dash Beardsley, the force behind Ghost Tours of Galveston, the reason Galveston is considered one of the most haunted cities in the United States is the Island's unique timeline of tragedy. "Yes, Galveston has seen more than its fair share of death, but the Great Storm of 1900 was just the crescendo of things," he said. "The history of death on the Island goes back much further."

The Karankawa Indians were the first known Islanders who terrified (and at times enslaved) European adventurers crazy enough to withstand mosquito ambush and melting temperatures to try and civilize what was then just an sandbar. "They were ritualistic cannibals," said Beardsley. "The Karankawa would eat their enemies to keep them from reaching the third heaven, their idea of paradise."

Centuries old newspaper archives about the Karankawa give much less mystical reasons for the Indian's cannibalistic behavior. "What incurable optimists those bold Spanish missionaries must have been to select the Karankawa ogres of the Gulf as subjects for conversion to Christianity," said one writer from the *Houston Post* in 1933. "They were all barbarians, given to idleness…they were lazy, indolent. They were very gluttonous and ravenous and ate meat almost raw, roasted, and dripping with blood."

On killing a member from another tribe: "They threw this savage on the prairie: one cut his throat, and on his arms, while one took off his skin. Several at the flesh, which was cut raw, and then they devoured him entirely."

On their refusal to become Christians: "All but a few had forsaken the great spirit of the Spaniards and returned to their ancient pagan gods, whom they worshipped on the beach sands and forests, beneath a gibbous moon, with their terrible all night mitotes – fantastic, drunken ceremonial dances around

28

campfires accompanied by the eerie music of shrieks, moans, and writhings, enlivened by cannibal feasts."

In 1528, after weeks at sea, the starving-to-death Spaniards found a seemingly empty camp near what is now called "Three Trees" on the far West end of the Island. As the men looked up from their feasting, they were surrounded by what Cabeza de Vaca described in his diary as "tall, naked, well-formed men" who were also equipped with giant bows and arrows pointed directly at them.

The Karankawa – true to Galveston form – were rare and even a bit exclusive. Characteristic of Nomads, they kept to themselves, especially from other Indian tribes. In 1934 the *Houston Post* referred to them as the "Ishmaelites of Texas, for their hands were against every man, and every man's hands were against them...they were continually at war with other tribes."

Roasting fish caught at sea (courtesy Library of Congress)

In the early 1930s, archaeologists found human bones on Bolivar Peninsula believed to be the "remains of cannibalistic festivities." In 1962, excavators discovered a Karankawa burial site on Jamaican Beach. Experts continue to find Karankawan artifacts, primarily on Jamaican Beach, to this day.

Historians disagree about the purpose of the Karankawa's cannibalistic ways, though most agree they did practice some level of ritualistic cannibalism, possibly connected to their lack of resources and harsh existence. "They lived without agriculture and few tools; they lived uncomfortably at the mercy of nature," wrote David G. McComb in *Galveston: A History*.

By the mid-1800s the remaining Karankawa who had not "...gone onto their reward in the Happy Hunting Ground because of white man's boots, bullets, booze, and bacteria," as the *Houston Post* put it, were believed to have migrated to Mexico on canoes, vanishing into oblivion forever.

Or have they?

Perhaps the spirits of the Karankawa – and the spirits of those they killed – continue to roam the Island, their Nomadic ways enduring beyond the illusion of time. Certainly the survive-no-matter-what attitude endures in the resilient nature of Islanders, along with a territorial protectiveness sometimes vigilant, other times bordering on the possessive.

Dash Beardsley speaks of Galveston's geographical location as contributing to its haunted nature, referring to the Island as being located in a "mysterious spot." "Water attracts energy," he said.

Like the story of the Zeus's wife Hera being hung in the sky and bound by golden chains by her angry husband's thunderbolt, the Karankawa's place in Galveston history possesses the qualities of a myth – nothing to be taken too literally. In fact, in the book *The Karankawa Indians of Texas* by Robert A. Ricklis, the author dispels the belief that the

Karankawa were savage cannibals who ate human flesh for satiation. "Yes, they sometimes ate the captured enemy warriors and leaders after a battle or war. They did not do this for food. They did it to get the magic power of the dead warrior or leader."

He forgives this act by making a comparison to their peers, as "Almost every other Texas Indian tribe did the same thing."

In sharp contrast to his documentarian predecessors, Ricklis writes about the Karankawa's interactions with the first Europeans to land on the Island, a version of the history so dichotomous to those originals works, you finish reading wondering if history is not only unfair, but has the nature of the relationship between Europeans and Indians exactly opposite.

"When the Spanish explorer Cabeza de Vaca was shipwrecked on Galveston Island in 1528, the Karankawa treated him very well. They gave de Vaca and his companions food, shelter, and support. Cabeza de Vaca gives us the first recorded, and one of the better, accounts about the Karankawa. De Vaca lived with one of the Karankawa bands for several years and joined the band."

In Ricklis's writings, the Karankawa are painted as guides and supporters to the destitute Spanish, rather than predators. Considering the Karankawa began dying from imported disease at an exponential rate soon after de Vaca's arrival, along with the fact that both Spanish and French coast cruisers had made a habit out of kidnapping and enslaving the Island Indians, and stealing their canoes, a certain level of skepticism is necessary to gain a fuller and fairer understanding of these Island nomads.

Some accounts go on to suggest that perhaps it was the Spanish, in their starving, shipwrecked alarm and desperation, who introduced the unsettling notion of cannibalism, rather than the other way around.

Alvar Nunez Cabeza de Vaca (courtesy Library of Congress)

Subversive threads of racism have historically influenced how content is remembered. Opposition is wound through mythology, and in this light, the story of the Karankawa gathers like fish in Poseidon's Great Sea. Despite their elusive history, one thing is for sure: like Galvestonians themselves, the Karankawa were a misunderstood people. And there is magic in the mystery.

Whether the Karankawa ate human flesh in order to ingest their spirit, had no choice, or were influenced by the Spaniards, no one can deny the Karankawa were the first humans in Galveston's history. The Karankawas could have opened up a spiritual portal for the thousands of Islanders who would perish by the treacherous hands of nature and man in the years to come. Their greatest contribution was in setting an important Galveston standard – to endure, to live despite – perhaps in spite of – the havoc of storm, the pestilence of mosquito, and the judgment of the world on the other side of the water.

Jean Lafitte & the Sea-Raiding Community of Galveston

Gulfbase.org, a "resource database for Gulf of Mexico research," informs the public about the unique character of cities located on the water: "Coastal areas are among the most important places in the world to live and locate industry." Coastal cities, with their complex systems of bayous, canals, channels and small embayments, possess the capacity for things landlocked cities cannot, like commercial fishing, recreational tourism, oil and gas development, and international import and exporting.

Barateria Bay, in Jefferson Parish on the Louisiana Coast, is the lifeblood to migratory birds who utilize its swamps and marshes as a nursery. Like a nest, the wetlands provide privacy and protection from outsiders, perfect for breeding and parenting. Inland bays like Barateria are also perfect locations for less cycle-of-life acts, even illicit activities like smuggling goods. And people.

Enter Jean Lafitte.

In 1811, Barateria was to smugglers what New York City Italian family-run restaurants are to the mafia in movies like *The Godfather*: a sanctuary for lawlessness. When a tall, mustachioed man with an aquiline nose stepped his booted foot on wetlands' swallowing soil, a star was made.

Authorities knew him as Jean Lafitte, a proud Frenchman. Along with older brother Pierre, Jean abandoned his Royal Street warehouse just as the French La Vieux Carre transitioned into the American French Quarter. The Americans and their tariffs made New Orleans much less appealing to the young entrepreneur.

To say Jean Lafitte was an opportunist is like saying Bourbon Street has a lot of drunks.

Within an impressively short amount of time, Jean was running Barateria Bay, and running it with the managerial capacity of a symphony conductor. Because of all the multitudinous needs met by his non-taxed goods and services (including the illegal import of slaves), he became, as biographer Jack C. Ramsay put it in his book *Jean Lafitte: Prince of Pirates*, not only a highly sought after man in New Orleans, but in time gained the admiration befitting royalty, titled the "...the uncrowned prince of the kingdom by the sea."

Jean's reputation as "a man who can get things" might have helped his case with the Americans. With the British approach, and without an organized navy to speak of, the Americans were anxious. Still, General Andrew Jackson questioned the Americans' proposed alliance with the inhabitants at the Bay against the Brits in the Battle of New Orleans in 1814: "I ask you, Louisianans, can we place any confidence in the honor of men who have courted an alliance with pirates and robbers?" nicknaming the smugglers at Barateria Bay "hellish banditti."

Jackson had a change of heart after actually meeting the esteemed privateer. Like many great men who at one point or another interacted with Jean Lafitte, the future president respected Jean's zest for the fight. Jean seemed to the General unphased by all that protecting American soil in a war primarily played out at sea sans navy, required.

When the Lafitte brothers and their "hellish banditti" showed up at the General's headquarters on Royal Street, it was a scene from a big-budget Johnny Depp movie: a motley crue of men of multiple races, ages, and nationalities, proclaiming their loyalty to the Americans, under the leadership of a man with the unusual dichotomy of being both unsettling and captivating, like a snake. There was only one condition – and with Jean there was always a condition – that General Jackson request a pardon for every man who fought.

The General accepted.

Jean Lafitte's ability to procure arms and war materials during the Battle of New Orleans was to General Jackson as a prison supplier is to a jailhouse junkie: utterly indispensable. The American government watched on the sidelines like a sickly cheerleader, either unable or unwilling to supply Louisiana with the assistance they needed. The Americans simply couldn't deny the privateer's offer to step in.

Jean Lafitte's life can be defined by his consistent willingness to fulfill a need.

Still it was a surprise when the Brits began their journey back over the Atlantic – Americans the victor. According to biographer Jack Ramsay, after the Lafitte brothers and their Baratcria bandits successfully helped win for America the battle over the Louisiana territory, General Andrew Jackson had nothing but praise for them "...in particular two brave men who 'exhibited the same courage and fidelity…the government shall be duly appraised of their conduct.'"

Jean Lafitte's lifelong commitment to his own free agency served him like a girl scout selling cookies. Even high ranking officials and law-enforcing authorities bought into what Jean represented, and as much as he might have been – *should* have been – incarcerated for his diehard shunning of the law, those same attributes which made him a successful pirate made him an irresistible addition to the cause, whatever the *cause* happened to be. General Jackson's praise rang like an international recommendation.

In 1815, already five years into the war to free Mexico from Spain – the Mexican War of Independence – the Spanish were growing desperate. Perhaps it was desperation prompting them to write a contract with the Lafitte brothers, hiring them as spies to be stationed on this yet-to-be-claimed island on the edge of southeast Texas. Pierre and Jean – two people who had for a time pirated Spanish ships – *now worked for the Spanish Crown*. Should there be any question as to the luck, charisma, and capacity for eclecticism of Jean Lafitte, one only has to look back into history.

Jean Lafitte first arrived on Galveston Island on a tour of espionage, specifically assigned to the Mexican revolutionary and Commodore Louis Michel-Aury. This largely uninhabited sandbar known to the French as *San Louis Island*, named by French explorer Sieur de La Salle, when he landed there by mistake in 1685, was renamed *Galvezton* by Spanish navigator Jose Antonio de Evia for his benefactor the viceroy of Mexico Bernardo de Galvez in 1762, and the Mexicans as *Campeche,* after a city in Mexico.

But for Jean Lafitte, one must understand that even espionage is too obvious a task. San Louis Island / Galvezton / Campeche might have been full of mosquitoes and aggressive Indians called the Karankawa, but as it was outside of

American jurisdiction and harboring its own inland bay, it was also an ideal port.

Jean had serendipitously discovered a new and improved Barateria.

To get a sense of what Jean must have been thinking upon his initial Island arrival, one must think like a pirate. Or painter. Imagine Picasso and a blank canvas. On the outside his expression remains stoic; nothing is yet removed from reality. Inside neurons fire like Jean Lafitte's Battle of New Orleans cannon. With swiftness he maneuvers, as natural and inevitable an act as breathing.

Colors slide back and forth like oily waves, misshapen like carnival playhouse reflections. Outside, the landscape – once fierce and empty – explodes into a barroom brawl of color, exactly correct for what it is, which is to say not correct at all; the mismatched perfection of unconventional paradigms. Outside is revolution of the spirit. But it is also something more. It is something being born.

Jean Lafitte in Galveston.

Jean accomplished his duties and more. After gaining the confidence of Louis Aury, Jean and Pierre reported back to Spain. According to Jack Ramsay, Jean's trustworthiness, despite having pirated Spanish ships, was upheld by the man in charge of gathering data for the Spanish in Cuba. Felipe Fatio's glass-is-half-full perspective was ultimately convincing enough for the Spanish Crown. "...they [Pierre and Jean] had been charitable 'not only toward the Spanish taken as prisoners by their boats, but also other captives.'"

Pierre and Jean were considered trustworthy even though they had formerly pirated ships because *they had been friendly toward their captives*. The fact that the brothers had at one time emptied Spanish vessels of all valuables was only incidental.

This, the magic of Jean Lafitte.

The Pirate Jean Lafitte

Jean gave two promises: one to Spain that he was still watching out for their best interest, and one to Louis Aury – the man for whom he was sent to spy – promising the same. Aury, as it turned out, was not a Mexican Revolutionary but one of Jean Lafitte's own, a man with whom Jean could truly empathize: an enterprising, sea raiding, pirate.

Just as Jean promised Spain he would maintain order on the Island, he promised Aury he would maintain order until Aury's return to Campeche. Jean did make good on this promise, with one minor but lane-changing caveat – he completely took over control of the Island, putting himself in charge, his motley crue of bandittos following his lead in the way only criminals can… with absolute abandon.

Jean began updating Galveztown, replacing Aury's makeshift huts with proper buildings, anchored into the sand with solid posts. Jean's makeover efforts reflected those of a pioneer establishing a new colony on barren land, if that pioneer also acted as dictator, overseeing any and all operations, requiring complete subordination, including an oath of allegiance from each newcomer. Houses, hotels, and bars (of course) sprang up like wild daisies, seemingly out of nowhere and angling toward the sun.

Jean convinced New Orleans he was busy establishing a "new government" in Galveston, and that his efforts and time spent there all but for the greater good of his Louisiana alma mater. To Spain he maintained the illusion of Enforcer, and to the Americans he was simply outside of control. Jean ran Galveston Bay with the same puppeteering panache he had Barateria – except this time with even greater ambition.

Galveston spread out like Zeus's bedroll compared to its shy counterpart to the East, and uncolonized, one whose Mexican flag waved with the wilting dispassion of a marriage of convenience. It soon became apparent to the world that this hero of the Battle of New Orleans – this charismatic pirate whose name requires a French accent to be properly pronounced – now possessed the 28 mile sandbar along the Gulf of Mexico the way a cat possesses a spot of sun on the ground; as though that spot was created just for him, and he was entitled to it.

Jean had come into his own.

Like any self-aggrandizing king, Jean built himself a throne. He painted it the color of blood and called it Maison Rouge. From the sea the house appeared like a formidable stronghold, but there was something exotic about the place, something unexplainably wild. Like a dragonfruit, the contents of Maison Rouge were as juicy as they were unattainable.

Maison Rouge was the missing piece to Jean's story, a material manifestation of his life, possibly contrived to fuel the blazing fire of his infamy, but still, a symbol. If a pirate could live in a mansion on a barren island and paint it bright red, anything is possible.

An anything-is-possible attitude is required in order to accept the next chapter in Jean Lafitte's story. Because unlike the myths and legend conjured by the silver screen, Jean Lafitte was not always the embodiment of Underdog Hero, not wasn't always the likeable criminal, someone the audience loves to love. No, Jean Lafitte was a true opportunist, and so when the universe brought to him this bizarre convergence, he had no choice but to yari it with the gouging finesse of a feudal samurai.

Site of Lafitte's Maison Rouge

Diving head-first into the deep end of the slave trade was less a reflection of his political and ethical notions as it was his foundational ones; he was a pirate, after all. It wasn't that he felt unfavorably toward the Africans. In fact all signs pointed to the contrary; the bandittos reflected nothing if not a global palette.

In April 1818, when the American Congress passed a bill putting a stop to illegal slave importation, offering half the market value of any Africans discovered on board a ship, they unwittingly opened the door for massive – albeit shameful – profit margins for the Island's lead pirate.

Jean ordered his raiders to strong-arm any vessel carrying would-be slaves in the Gulf. Plantation owners from Louisiana caught word and conducted business with Jean with the hunger and ease of a grazing cow. Jean's men were much too adept at their duties, and the overflow of slaves was sent across ferries and miles of treacherous land to the United States.

The so-called slave runners would hand the laborers over to the U.S. Marshals, accept the monetary reward, purchase the slaves back at auction, only to sell them again to the highest bidding Louisiana plantation.

The blasphemous inhumanity of this dishonorable system cannot be understated. Countless men died during the journey from the Island on behalf of Jean Lafitte's greed. The men who survived were no luckier than their fallen countrymen.

So as it is with the universe, Jean Lafitte's luck was about to take a turn.

Despite his obvious ethical failures, Lafitte never failed his old world gentility. A woman who lived on the island journaled about her experiences there, emphasizing her feelings of security, as Jean mandated that "anyone who molested a married woman would be hanged."

Looming in the distance was a new foe – the United States Navy – eyeing the pseudo civilization Jean Lafitte had created with the pinched craving of a starved wolf.

Despite Jean's ability to stave off the impending powers-that-be, the American Navy was itching to flex their new muscles, as the slave trade weakened to a diminished nothing. The colony the pirate had built waned like the shallow water of an outgoing tide.

And so in the winter of 1821, Jean's schooner set sail once again, leaving behind the ruins of his kingdom forever.

To understand Jean Lafitte – to see the details of him – the person he was, the incomprehensible details of his life, his mischievous genius, his damaged self, his fierce, frothing-at-the-mouth defense in the name of Freedom and Independence, his snake-charming ways, is to grasp the spirit of island he knew as Eureka. If you know the story of Jean Lafitte you begin to understand the complicated relationship between Galveston's unique character and its bloody past, why Galveston is one of the most inimitable, most surprising, and most haunted cities in the world.

Jean Lafitte Historical Marker at Maison Rouge site

Matilda – The Lesser Known
Ghost of Ashton Villa

In a *New York Times* article by Robert Reinhold, "Galveston, a 19th Century Island City," the elusive qualities of towns like Galveston is explained: "There is something about cities on islands that sets them apart from other places, temperamentally as well as geographically. They are insular, inbred and – fortunately, in many ways – resistant to the homogenizing social and economic forces that have blended most other modern cities into one undifferentiated mass."

Galveston is certainly isolated, but the word 'isolation' doesn't cover it. "The causeway that leads across Galveston Bay to the long narrow barrier island is like a time machine transporting the visitor into a 19th-century world of light and airy Victorian, Gothic and Greek Revival buildings and homes," Reinhold wrote.

Architecturally, Galveston is most obviously a "19th Century Island City," with the mansions on Broadway looming silent and serious and proud, like museum pieces. Among them is Ashton Villa, a restored 1859 3-story brick museum centerpiece (one of the first brick homes in Texas) run by Galveston's esteemed preservation organization, the Galveston Historical Foundation (GHF).

To fully appreciate the significance of a successful restoration project such as Ashton Villa, one must appreciate the significance of Island history.

After the Texas Revolution in 1835, the Texas Navy made the Port of Galveston its home, and two years later it became a port of entry to the Republic of Texas. Ten years later Galveston became a port of entry to the United States when the great Republic was republic no more. A critical inclusion for the American South, as supplies trickled in for the Confederate soldiers. In the late 19th Century, Galveston was one of the busiest ports in the country. During this period of Galveston history, many firsts were introduced to the Lone Star State:

Galveston proudly boasts the first:

- *naval base (1836)*
- *bakery (1838)*
- *chapter of the Masonic Order (1840)*
- *military company (1841)*
- *cotton compress (1842)*
- *law firm west of the Mississippi River (1846)*
- *Catholic convent (1847) & first Cathedral (1847)*
- *grocery store (1851)*
- *railroad locomotive (1852)*
- *insurance company (1854)*
- *use of telegraph (1854)*

- *private bank (1854)*
- *jewelry store (1856)*
- *gas lights (1856)*
- *real estate firm (1857)*
- *hospital and trade union (1866)*
- *drug store, Star Drug Store (1867, still in operation)*
- *opera house (1870)*
- *cotton exchange (1872)*
- *orphanage (1876)*
- *telephone (1878)*
- *electric lights (1883)*
- *medical college (1886)*
- *electric street cars (1893)*
- *school for nurses (1894)*
- *golf course (1898)*
- *country club (1898)*
- *Jewish Reform Congregation (1868)*

Between 1838 and 1842, 18 newspapers were started. *The Galveston News*, founded in 1842, is the only surviving newspaper now published as *The Galveston County Daily News*. It is the oldest daily newspaper in the state. A bridge to the mainland was completed in 1860.

By 1900, Galveston was one of the fastest growing cities in the United States.

But that all changed on September 8, 1900. Simply put, the Great Storm made Galveston a ghost town. Literally.

"Ghosts are energy, just like us," wrote *New York Times* bestselling author James Van Praagh in his book *Ghosts Among Us*. "Ghosts tend to show up when death was sudden and unexpected, and the deceased are unaware of their condition, or when death was traumatic like from a storm."

With all this death relative to Galveston's small size, might the Island be a "perfect storm" for paranormal activity – a sort of community center for ghosts – those curious entities whose energy vibrates too fast to see, whose deaths were instantaneous, unanticipated and ultimately unaccepted?

Whether it is this "mysterious" location, or a result of a laundry list of tragedy, Galvestonians possess the right attitude for a ghost town. There is palpable pride in the voice of a business owner as he speaks about the friendly ghost who appears as he's closing for the night. There is an openness about the Islanders, a non-discriminating, welcoming spirit-to-the-spirits. Simply put: Galvestonians love their ghosts.

And Islanders fight for their historic properties; Galveston has one of the best historical archives in the state. In this way, crossing over the causeway is like entering a portal.

A favorite amongst tourists – Ashton Villa – appears like a dollhouse as traffic screeches and turns on busy Broadway, each room made up for its invisible dwellers – the Island's most beloved ghost, Bettie Brown.

Everybody knows the stories about Bettie... Bettie Brown, the infamous ghost of Ashton Villa. Bettie Brown, the fiercely independent woman of the 1800s whose adventurous inclinations triumphed over domestic pressures. Bettie Brown, the woman who never married, who lived in Ashton Villa until her death.

But who was Matilda, and why might she be the ghost haunting Galveston's beloved Broadway mansion instead of her more well-known sister?

Ashton Villa was built by James Brown, the family's patriarch in 1859, after Brown's success in the hardware business, which makes Ashton Villa the first mansion built on Broadway. Brown designed the house to look like an Italian villa, gated by distinctive Mediterranean wrought iron swirls.

In the 1800s, Broadway was a dirt road of Victorian mansions, delicate in feature, monstrous by design.

Ashton Villa has a history of standing apart. Even today, the Villa is unique in that it is the only Antebellum mansion on Broadway.

"There were many deaths in Ashton Villa," said Jami Durham, Events Organizer for GHF and former Assistant Director for Historic Properties. "Both Mr. and Mrs. Brown died in the house, as did Bettie."

Unlike Bettie, Matilda, the youngest of the Browns' five children, did not travel the world, instead suffering through an abusive marriage. While Bettie Brown is the name cited in stories of haunted Ashton Villa, it is Matilda who ultimately made Jami Durham a Believer.

"There are three incidences which stand out in my mind," said Durham. "Two of these can possibly find a rational explanation, but one cannot."

Ashton Villa, compared to other Broadway mansions, is comparatively humble in size, though no less dramatic. The floor-to-ceiling windows punctuating the brick walls seem to invert harsh light like a jewel; daylight becomes dappled yellow glitter, but the impact is less in color than emphasis on sound, or lack thereof.

The front Gold Room looks like a movie set – each detail down to the food mirroring not just a time period out of reach, but a way of life. It is as if Bettie Brown is forever hosting a lavish party for a small gathering of international friends – fun (if not a bit disconcerting) to imagine as she watches you from her outsized portrait over the front hall's magnificent stairway.

What is less easy to imagine is the suffering of her younger sister, whose abusive husband ultimately forced her exodus to Ashton Villa.

Jami Durham recalls recreating Matilda's wedding reception: "We labored over the details," she said. "Even the

47

wedding cake. I worked very hard to make that wedding reception come alive again."

Durham's attention to detail worked to a startling degree. "I was standing there facing the Gold Room when out of nowhere a white flash of light whizzed by. It was so real, my colleague and I assumed it was someone from the tour. We even called to the person aloud. When we realized no one was there, we simply could not believe it. Was it Matilda responding to her staged wedding reception? I don't know. But whatever it was, it felt very real."

Portrayal of Matilda on the Stairs

48

In addition to recreating the home of a wealthy 19th Century family for museum guests, Durham was also responsible for meeting the security alarm company every time an alarm unexpectedly sounded.

Beautiful Ashton Villa

When heirloom family furniture was laboriously retrieved from Louisiana and placed just inside the backdoor the alarm sounded three different times through the night. "Security checked the perimeter each time and found nothing. There simply is no reason for that alarm to have gone off." Durham says she was again awoken in the middle of the next night. Again, the security team found nothings- no breaks in windows, no opened doors, and absolutely no humans. A funny thing happened, however, when the furniture was at last returned to its rightful owners, the Browns.

"When we were finally able to move the furniture into the house, the alarms suddenly stopped. I think the family was anxious about this missing piece of furniture, and seeing it just beyond their reach created much activity."

If ghosts are restless spirits, than doesn't it make more sense for Matilda to be the one whose steps bounce echoes off the walls of Ashton Villa rather than her more liberated, restful, sister?

Perhaps the only way to know is to cross over onto the isolated waters of this real-life ghost town, take a tour of Ashton Villa, and decide for yourself.

The Lobby of the Tremont House From a Bygone Era
(Courtesy of Rosenberg Library)

Hauntings and History
at the Tremont

The Tremont House is a porcelain doll. Painted the most delicate shade of pink, pieced together with meticulous care, displayed as art, and put back together every time its painfully exquisite, fragile parts are destroyed. The Tremont is also prized as a museum piece, especially by those who value grandiose pronouncements – this obsessive human need to be surrounded by beautiful things. Obsessive humans – this is what keeps Tremont thriving, and what makes it one of the most haunted hotels on the Island.

Like many famous structures in Galveston, the Tremont is not an original. The current model is its third version, a middle child between extreme opulence and humility.

On San Jacinto Day in 1839, the first Tremont opened its doors to the public. From the start the hotel made headlines, though it was only a "...sturdy, two-story building," as described by the *Austin Business Journal*.

But the hotel was also the biggest in all of Texas, and already a beckoning stage for those seeking the spotlight. In his last public speech, General Sam Houston stood boldly on the balcony of the brand new hotel and addressed a hostile crowd, just after secession from the Union was officially announced, warning that "fires and rivers of blood" would come as a result.

In the heat of the summer of 1865, the first of many Galveston fires ravaged downtown; by the end of the day the Tremont was a sifting heap of crispy, black ashes.

Seven years later the famous Galveston architect of the late 19th Century Nicholas Clayton was hired to rebuild what was considered – thanks to General Houston's riveting words – a landmark.

In 1872 one of the grandest hotels in the entire nation was born, boasting four storerooms, a barbershop, billiards room, saloon, European style showpiece lobby, and the latest of inventions – a steam-powered elevator, "...a convenience by which guests are conveyed to upper stories."

And that was just the first floor.

Until the Great Storm, the hotel maintained its elite status. When Ulysses S. Grant visited the Island, a grand banquet was held in his honor. In 1928, the *Galveston Daily News* wrote about the discovery of a register of famous visitors to Tremont's observatory, or "look-out tower," including the names of six presidents, a gaggle of celebrities, and "...every person who figured on the front page of the newspapers in that decade."

The Saloon of the old Tremont House (Courtesy of Rosenberg Library)

The 1900 Storm sent hundreds of desperate people on the hike of their lives to the top floor, the glassy demonic waters below nipping at their feet. The Great Storm would ultimately take perhaps not all the lives of Galveston, but most certainly all its livelihood. Post 1900, the Tremont's lion-on-the-mountain status waned. Just before its demolition in 1928, the *Houston Chronicle* wrote: "What was formerly the pride of the South has been content to drowse in the shade, dreaming after the manner of old things." And that same day the "Final chapter in the eventful history of Tremont" was concluded.

Thanks to the great visionaries Cynthia and George Mitchell, the Tremont was once again reborn in the early 1980s, described by the *Houston Post* as "...running with the precision of a big city deluxe hotel."

And also unique. Anecdotal stories from guests and hotel employees, along with folklore, began to emerge, adding to its top notch reputation, an entirely new dimension.

After a series of knockings, the ceiling fan switching on and off, and a "...darkness pass the crack of light that was shining in from the curtain and less than a minute later... three low deep moans in our room very close to our faces," one hotel guest wrote of her family's 2009 stay at the hotel, "...I felt an unusual pain like a knife stabbed into my ribcage so I rolled over and it remained there and felt very real for at least five minutes. If I had been alone in that room I would have left it at that point... I have never been a believer in paranormal activity until now!"

Employees report unexplainable, albeit minor, happenings such as lights, TVs, and ceiling fans going on and off, in both occupied and empty rooms. An employee who worked in Guest Services for several years relates a few hair-raising stories, including one from a manager of another hotel who complained of his shower going on and off intermittently, "breathing" on his ear while he slept, and whispering of a man's voice. Paralegals on a major case complained about the petulant nature of the shower, as did the employee's sisters, who also reported feeling a "presence above her while she was sleeping."

What makes these haunted stories even more compelling is that they originated from the same location – the East Side of the 4th floor, the part of the hotel formerly the Belmont House, whose original brick façade still counters the stoic white and black marble lobby.

One of Ghost Tours of Galveston's copyrighted stories is that of a salesman with a limp leg who went out gambling one night, returned early after winning big, only to be murdered in his hotel room, his pile of cash – and his murderer – never to be seen again.

Just after reconstruction post Hurricane Ike, hotel guests on the 4th floor complained of having peculiar experiences, strikingly similar in nature. One night, the doors to their rooms shook, followed by a loud pound – like a knock – on the door, startling them awake. Then guests reported hearing strange, one-footed stomping in the hallway, accompanying a distinct dragging noise.

Ghost Tours of Galveston Founder Dash Beardsley says how the salesman was killed remains "unclear." However, two guests of Tremont sent Beardsley a CD with the recording of an Electronic Voice Phenomena (EVP). The chilling words *broke my neck* were captured.

Is the ghost of the salesman attempting to awaken people to the truth of how he was murdered? Is an unpunished death enough to keep a spirit agitated for more than a hundred years?

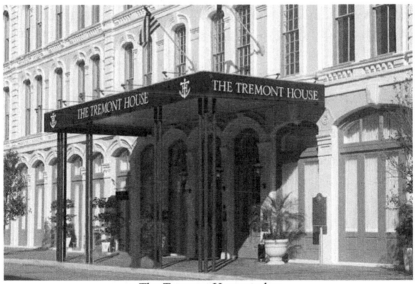

The Tremont House today

Galveston has a history of proving naysayers wrong. The words of the 1928 article by the *Houston Post* about the demolition of the Tremont may be poetic, but more poignant is the degree to which guests and employees of the Tremont would disagree: "The two Tremont hotels could write much of the story of Texas. One came to an abrupt end. The other withstood the Great Storm and played out its usefulness and now, even like the weariest river, it finally reaches the sea of oblivion."

To stand in the sun-dappled marbled lobby of the Tremont is to be oblivious only to what is improbable and forever endangered, to cultivate an appreciation for a time when luck existed on a continuum rather than a plateau, to stand in the center of a humble little island and feel truly romanced by a whirlwind of international luxury. If a hotel can withstand multiple fires, wars, and obliterating storms, there is no measure or standard higher for any architectural ingénue. This "Crown Jewel of Texas" will endure, as long as Islanders man its front desk, clean its floors, play its piano, and work to keep its spirit alive.

The Van Alstyne:
The Island's Most Haunted House?

On September 11, 1900, Rabbi Cohen of Galveston sent a telegraph message to the Governor of Texas, Joseph Draper Sayers:

```
Send military supplies, fire arms, animal human
food  stuff,  danger  food  riots  any  moment.
Situation  horrible;  cant  describe,  for  god  sake
help us.
```

Many books have been written about the infamous "Great Storm" of 1900. There were so many bodies survivors were forced to create makeshift funeral pyres in the middle of streets. The stench of the burning bodies is unimaginable; one newspaper headline read:

G a l v e s t o n   i s   D e a d.

While The Great Storm is to this day one of the most talked-about natural disasters in United States history, it was also "merely a crescendo of things," says Dash Beardsley, the force behind Ghost Tours of Galveston. Galveston had by 1900 already suffered massive loss. Epidemics like typhoid and yellow fever wreaked deathly tolls on Islanders.

Galveston's history of death goes back much further.

"I didn't believe in ghosts," Scottie Ketner, owner of upscale resale and antique shop Le Chat Noir said matter of factly. "But then I opened an antique business in an old Victorian house on Broadway I named Annabelle's, and let's just say my beliefs changed."

Annabelle's occupied the three-story Victorian mansion on 29th and Broadway in the mid-90s, a thriving co-op for several antique vendors. Ketner ignored the stories at first, despite the quality and quantity of them, until "...things started to happen."

"Alarms went off in the middle of the night, when no one was there. There was absolutely no reason for them to sound, but every time we redid a room in the house, they would go off repeatedly, to the point the officers coming to the scene knew with confidence they would find nothing and no one on the property."

"One time, two police officers arrived after being alerted by our system. One officer was a veteran – he had been out here before – but the other officer was new to the force. Or at least, that's how he seemed. They went up to the second floor and heard a noise. It was dead silent elsewhere in the house, so every little noise was noticeable. A toy truck suddenly came from one of the rooms and glided across the hall, which spooked the young officer. He drew his gun, but the other officer told him not to bother. 'We're not going to find anyone up here,' he told him.

A doll from the Annabelle days of the Van Alstyne House

And then we walked into a room and found one of my vendor's tables overturned. I followed the men, and was at first confused, when the young officer tried to hand me a $5 bill. Then I noticed the crucifix in his other hand, with a price tag of $4.95. He had put his gun away and replaced it with a cross from the shop. I guess he felt he needed a different kind of protection. I looked in his eyes and saw fear. He swore he could see someone behind one of the counters. I told him he could have the crucifix for free."

While the happenings on the second floor might have been enough to spook a police officer, it was what happened in the attic and the door leading up to it which made Ketner a believer. "The third floor was walled off when we moved in.

59

Which was strange." Though Ketner removed the wall she says all of us "experienced that door to the attic slamming shut at one point or another."

"There was something about the attic," she said. "I used to go up there when I needed a moment to myself. One time I experienced something truly bizarre. I was taking a rest when I heard this strange collection of voices of different European accents, and most definitely from another time."

"That place may be a portal," suggests Dash Beardsley, originator of Ghost Tours of Galveston, who numbers The Van Alstyne House as nine on his top ten most-haunted list. "Twice I saw a young man I believe was waiting for a lady. He might have been from a family who lived in the house. But he was very much there."

Ketner remembers the chilling anecdotes of former inhabitants of the house, who lived there when it was a youth shelter. With a certain wondrous glaze coming over them like a rescinding shadow, they inevitably asked her the same cryptic question, "Have you seen the man?"

One former inhabitant of the youth shelter told her a particularly back-of-the-neck hair-raising story. "He said he had gone to the third floor to find a game when he had the feeling he was being watched. He looked up to see a man in a dark, Victorian-era suit with a tall collar peering at him from the landing outside. Instinctively, the boy ran back downstairs, having recognized the fact that there was no landing outside on which the man could have been standing."

Not only was the house a 1900 Storm survivor, but according to the 1900 Storm map, which marks the areas of the island according to level of damage, the house received comparatively little damage; a remarkable fact, considering the utter devastation of the neighborhood immediately surrounding it.

Among the clutter of old papers on the third floor of the house, Ketner found a letter written by one of the original dwellers who had been in the house during the 1900 Storm, a Van Alstyne, who wrote: "Can you imagine 50 of us crammed underneath the stairs?" The letter also commented on the day's passing. The water was still too high for them to exit the house, and so, stuck inside, they "had nowhere else to look but through the window and count their blessings, as wagons of bodies passed by."

The Van Alstyne family was prominent in Galveston's beginnings. Patriarch of the family William Van Alstyne was featured on the front page of *The Galveston Daily News* in 1951 of a story entitled: "99 Years Since Invasion of Iron Horse in Texas," detailing Van Alstyne's participation in the building of Texas's first railroad. The article also mentions other important members of his family. "Perhaps the best authority on that railroad reputed to be the first west of the Mississippi, is Mrs. A.V. Harvey of 2901 Broadway, granddaughter of William Van Alstyne and daughter of the railroad pioneer's son Albert A. Van Alstyne who settled in Galveston..."

Albert managed of The National Cotton Oil Company, his wife Catherine, a world-renowned singer, was also featured on the front page of *The Galveston Daily News* in the 1930s. But being featured in the newspaper was nothing new for the family; the Van Alstynes were socialites, attending any event worth mentioning. They built the house in 1891 on Broadway, where grand Victorian mansions of upper crust Galvestonians lined the street with the audacious consistency of gas-lit lamp posts.

"The 1900 Storm, and the fact that the house was amongst so much rubble, could be the reason it is haunted to this day," Richard L. Smith, of Paranormal Investigations of Texas and author of *Everywhere I Go is Haunted*, stated. "You have to understand – there were thousands of bodies around Galveston for weeks after the storm. This could have been when the spirits of these people who died so tragically and unexpectedly, found a home at 2901 Broadway."

Smith, who studied the house for two months when it was the antique store The Gingerbread House, knows not only the unusual happenings at the house, but also the unusual people who haunted it. With a background in military intelligence, Smith is an expert in Electronic Voice Phenomenon, or EVP, the method paranormal investigators use in order to analyze the 'who' and the 'why' of alleged haunted spaces. A video of Smith contacting and recording a particularly diabolical male spirit who happened to be bothering the owner of the house can be seen on youtube.com. The video comes with parental caution.

Ketner never knew of any evil spirit and said she never felt in danger. "I felt very protected. In fact, [one time] a man I knew walked into the store while I was upstairs. I remember feeling inexplicably compelled to call out his name, as if to discover his whereabouts. Later, I realized he had been stealing from us. Had I not been overwhelmed with the need to call his name, we might not have caught him. And that was the one and only time we were vandalized. We never had any trouble from the neighborhood because people living around us were so afraid of the house that they stayed away!"

The house is no longer home to any business and remains under construction. The traffic on Broadway whizzes passed in an apathetic rush, but when you watch the house, the watching becomes a reflection, a portal to memory. That impossibly large, and slightly broken down, house on the end of the street. You know the one – it dares you to enter its gate, walk up to the stoop and peer in. It is surreal and alive, like a pop-up book, this house teeming with life, accessible to everyone, yet somehow able to remain incognito; much like Galveston itself.

Stewart's Mansion Entry Arch

Stewart's Mansion:
The City's Favorite Haunted Ruins

The Hindus believe the soul is immortal. *Carnate* means "flesh." *Rein* means to reinter. To the Hindus, those faithful followers of the world's oldest organized religion with the 3rd largest membership reaching up to a billion (just behind Islam and Christians), how one reinters the earth has everything to do with the life they lived. And there is a hierarchy.

Jean Lafitte and his pirates were not Hindus.

If the French "privateer," along with his own band of dutiful henchmen, had subscribed to the idea of reincarnation, perhaps they would have done things a little differently.

Here at Stewart's Mansion, not a day has passed. Ten miles out on the West side of the Island the archway beckons like the gold cap inside a pirate's mouth. It is as if Jean Lafitte chose the font himself – the masthead as much an invitation as a warning. Stewart's Mansion [Old English]. Beware. Come on in. Beware. Come on in.

The driving path leads the way, and you follow with eager concentration, like you're either on a ride at Epcot, or about to order a burrito. But even Disney couldn't create such perfection. Beams of wood slant downward, opening and shutting again, noticeable only by the sun's crooked journey across the sky.

Front of Stewart's Mansion

Diagonal bars of sunlight seems to glorify the invisible nothings – the air is empty and full like the past. Weeds and insects burrow in the dark crevices and grow out, indignant to unfamiliarity. Stairs lead to nowhere, a sort of swaying, and a courtyard to die for; blue tiles line a spidered fireplace tell the tale of knights and maidens – these are Spanish hieroglyphics – artist unknown.

A step down onto remnants of life – dirt, sand, dust, empty soda cans. More rooms and more rooms, the blue sky injects more menace to the contrast of light and dark than remedy. You expect a reaction to your sound and movement, or at least some loose board to break underneath, but there is nothing.

What was once a grand entryway – more stairs to nowhere. You are afraid to look, afraid if you wait too long and stand still for just a moment you will become a Believer.

Two murals. Men, fierce men. Long dark hair and weapons raised. Centerpieces missing from their faces as though someone – or something- had grown weary of them.

You step out the open space where a front door once shut the world away, and onto the extended shadows of a dead tree who speaks to you – *treasure is buried underneath the ruins.* Jean Lafitte's treasure. *But his wife is still there.* She is the 3-dimensional sucking blackness you passed on the way in – she is the quiet, unsatisfied expectation of your unfounded presence. Whatever transpires on her doorstep at night must cause pure, electric terror.

Treasure. With the U.S. Navy at his heels, Jean Lafitte knew his time as Pirate King had come to a blazing fire end. Years of sea-raiding had long ago furnished his beloved home Maison Rouge – way out on the other side of the Island. Surely he sailed the short distance between East and West – the mosquitoes and their fatal poison so abundant in the marsh – and those pesky Karankawa upset about the sudden disappearance of a few of their young women.

He sailed here, to the West side, he sailed. And fought them off, or more likely talked them down; this was Jean Lafitte the enigmatic, charismatic dictator of Galveztown, after all. He needed a hiding spot for the loot. Through his veins the sense of urgency throbbed like a jellyfish sting.

Interior Mural at Stewart's Mansion

There is no way of knowing if Jean Lafitte actually took up residence at Stewart's Mansion. The line of ownership reads like a who's who of Galveston history.

In the early 1800s Governor of San Antonio de Bexar Juan N. Seguin was granted a large league of land on the East end of Galveston on behalf of his lawyer, Michel Menard, just before Menard created the Galveston City Company and enabled Island civilization.

One time Secretary of War for the Republic of Texas Warren D.C. Hall purchased the property and was the first to build a house on it, where he lived with his wife until he died in 1867. What is interesting to note about Hall is his affiliation with Jean Lafitte. Hall was interviewed by Dr. J. O. Dyer who wrote a book about the early history of Galveston. The physical description of Lafitte by Hall was published in *The Galveston Daily News*:

He was six feet and two inches high, and his figure of remarkable symmetry, with feet and hands so small, compare with his large stature, as to attract attention. He received visitors with an easy air of welcome and profuse hospitality. He wore no uniform but dressed fashionably ...he spoke English correctly but with a marked French accent. He possessed superior conversational powers, and entertained his guests with the rehearsal of many amusing anecdotes. He had a remarkable habit of closing one eye while in conversation, and keeping it closed so much, that many who had but a slight acquaintance with him were firmly impressed with the belief that he had the use of but one eye.

Hall arrived on Bolivar Peninsula in a filibuster expedition in 1815. It is possible Lafitte attempted to bring Hall in on his privateering business, but as a respectable pioneer of Texas, Hall had no interest. However, Hall's public description of Lafitte indicates at least a fondness.

Hall named his home Three Trees, perhaps in recognition of the Battle of Three Trees, between the Karankawa and Lafitte's men in 1821, a battle whose details are as unclear as the Gulf of Mexico. What is clear is the genesis of the fight: women. Lafitte's bandittos apparently took a liking to the Karankawa women and captured a few along the way.

Regardless of the nature of the Battle of Three Trees, a historical link between Lafitte and the Stewart Mansion exists. More than likely Lafitte was a guest of the Colonel at Three Trees at one point or another. Who knows? Considering Lafitte's naughty tendencies, he might have been casing the joint. Or maybe he was just looking for a good hiding spot. No one before or since seems to have been able to find a better use for the place than burying treasure.

Maco Stewart, founder of Stewart Title, purchased the property in 1939 and donated it in 1944 to UTMB as a convalescent home for crippled children which closed only five years later. Since 1959 Stewart Mansion has been empty.

In 2008 the land was acquired by a developer called Lafitte's Harbor Development, with plans of building a gated townhouse community with the mansion as the community center. Four years later the land is still unused, the mansion dilapidated but not obliterated. With no gate, no signs and no security whatsoever, the mansion remains a most strange phenomenon. There is no historic landmark sign in front, and while Galveston Historical Foundation (GHF) included the property on its Heritage At Risk List in 2004, they have never owned the land, an act which surely would mean a second life for the starving mansion.

The Courtyard at Stewart's Mansion

The Internet is clogged with haunted stories in the way of blogs and articles, ranging from the wild and ridiculous – Maco Stewart killed his family and stuffed their bodies into the walls – to the spooky, as a blogger wrote about climbing the stairs to nowhere only to be stopped in his tracks by a "weird feeling" and a whispering voice.

The Islander Magazine published an article about Stewart's Mansion quoting the caretaker's warning to Roberta Marie Christensen, who took a tour of the ruins while doing research for her book *Pioneers of West Galveston Island*: "There are ghosts in [this] house, the caretaker told her. "My wife and I hear doors banging and noises in the middle of the night."

Many of the haunted stories surround the entryway murals. The two pirates are said to exchange places at night.

Former caretaker Jerry D. Penn admits that "Some reputable people claim to experience indubitable paranormal events while visiting the property."

It is easy to imagine. Surrounding the house are oak trees, but they are dead. Branches like fingers on a witch's hand, bent forward and back and straight down at the top, as though clasping down on something with violent intentions. Barren of life the oaks are tangible reminders of mortality, and here at Stewart's Mansion, mortality feels worse than death, like the morning after Brazil's legendary street party Carnaval. If what the Hindus believe is true, Lafitte's soul could still exist here in another form.

You keep the Hindu belief in reincarnation in mind as you muddle through the ruins. You look for living things – could Lafitte have turned into a butterfly or a sparrow? With the exception of the murals the ruins seem so colorless, so gray, so unlike Jean Lafitte. You step into the courtyard and find the giant surprise of a great, green palm extending its thick arms over the ground providing a universe of blissful shade.

An oak. Just as alive as the small black bat flapping his wings in rapid fire over the open doorway. You think about the hierarchy of Hindu afterlife. You wonder which of the two living things might be Jean Lafitte.

You think of Galveston. If Galveston could choose just one person from history to represent them, who would it be? Someone like Michel Menard, a man's man, a friend to all, a man who enjoyed living large and saw in Galveston great potential? Or might it be someone more like Samuel May Williams, a man who watched ships in the dark in the hopes of making a quick buck or two?

You decide neither. If given a choice, Galveston would choose someone like Jean Lafitte as their icon, a man who buried treasure, fought over women and impressed great men. A man possessing the qualities of both an oak tree, and a bat.

Stewart Mansion's Outside Stairs

Galveston's elegant Hotel Galvez (courtesy Atriad Press)

Hotel Galvez: Hauntings of the Rich & Infamous

It was 1915. Galveston lunged forward in the wake of a near apocalyptic storm 15 years prior. And now here it was all happening again – temperamental partners wind and rain in angry head-on collision, unleashing the sort of violence all too familiar to the Island. But there was something critically different about this hurricane. It had been patient, had been gracious enough to wait for the end of the Seawall's construction to begin its only marginally deadly assault.

Instead of flailing urgent and desperate arms, the city waited too, though inside the newly constructed Hotel Galvez the city danced. During a time when men wore chain-linked pocket watches and women full lengths gowns as a matter of course, the halls of the hotel echoed with the capricious music of a live band, harmonically overwhelming the clap-clap of palm fronds throttling outside. The spray of saltwater must have met the arched panes of hotel windows with a paintball splatter, but no matter. The gala lasted until the storm was over, and when the guests remembered the night, it wasn't flooding and fear they would discuss, it was the icy champagne and general magnificence of it all, focusing on not what might have been a devastating reality, but what was – when it was all said and done – just a whole lot of fun.

This is Galveston.

Fast forward to 1930. Sam Maceo serving highballs of whiskey and gin to Hollywood guests in his penthouse suite atop the Hotel Galvez, just across the Seawall from his booming business – the infamous Balinese Room – where there might have *possibly* been a bit of illegal gambling and boozing. The Maceos, with their indistinct Mafioso ties, spurred an economic upturn on the Island due to their bold entrepreneurial endeavors, an era known as Galveston's "Free State Years." And business, well business was good.

Though the Maceos and their Balinese Room were local legends, Hotel Galvez welcomed its share of global icons, such as rat packers Frank Sinatra, Sammy Davis Jr., and Dean Martin. Duke Ellington and Howard Hughes were hotel guests. Hughes, whose eccentricity and self-imposed isolation from the rest of mankind, did not keep him from enjoying weeks of room service in the glassy hotel's penthouse suite. President Lyndon B. Johnson's stay put the hotel on the political map; President Franklin Roosevelt made the hotel his official "Summer White House," indulging in ten days of fishing and general Island R&R.

When Hotel Galvez opened its doors in 1911, it was called a "symbol of survival" and introduced to Galveston the modern world. The hotel advertised the first of its kind potato peeling machine, icemaker, dishwasher, ice cream maker, concrete wine cellar, and printing press. The Seawall was a string of trendy bathhouses, and when The Galvez debuted, the event became the most poignant and lasting mark of the tourism industry, ultimately and permanently redefining the Island.

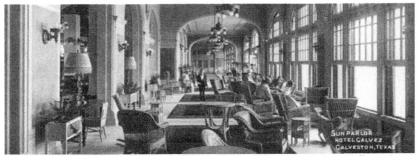

The Sun Parlor of the Hotel Galvez (Courtesy of Rosenberg Library)

This is a history not quite as well known as the hotel's paranormal side. While the hotel's hauntings have been the subject of countless bloggers and ghost-loving websites, what makes the attention The Galvez has received distinct from other Galveston favorites is that its stories have piqued the interest of even the mainstream news. ABC, the Travel Channel, and the Discovery Channel have all featured Haunted Galvez. A quick web search yields multiple entries about the hotel, the majority of hits illuminating a more ethereal theme in the hotel's story.

The most well known of Hotel Galvez's hauntings is the legend of the suicidal bride named Audra. The "Ghost Bride" was engaged to a mariner. Every night she would climb to the turrets on the roof and watch and wait for her man's ship. But he didn't return. Night after night she climbed to the top of the hotel and searched into the darkness, as someone might search in blindness for light. When she was told his ship was lost at sea, the night following she climbed the spiraling turrets not to search but to die.

Her room 501 is now requested by hapless guests, ghost hunters and the vaguely curious so often that the hotel must frequently turn disappointed callers away. Guests and hotel employees report enough unexplainable incidents for the hotel to lead the pack as the singularly most well documented haunted property on an island of haunted properties.

A bygone days photograph of the Dining Room of the Hotel Galvez
(Courtesy of Rosenberg Library)

Stories told on the web from former guests possess a particularly engaging authenticity, as the writers relate their tales from an innocuous perspective. These are just regular tourists who were anxious for a relaxing weekend at a nice hotel – these are not ghost hunters searching for validation. From a writer on Trip Advisor: "Two nights in a row we had a strange occurrence. The phone rang, we'd pick up, and nothing but dial tone. This happened two nights in a row, three times each night. The front desk said no one had called. Come to think of it, that was a pretty cool paranormal experience…"

And from another Trip Advisor member without any apparent ghost-hunting agenda: "After I put my 3 small children to bed and got our bags unpacked I turned out the light and got in bed, no reason to feel any alarm. Then suddenly the speaker button on the room phone turned on and a dial tone filled the room. I immediately felt afraid and turned on the light. After turning the speaker phone off and finally talking myself into turning the lights off again it happened all over again. It wasn't until I actually told "it" to stop and prayed aloud for God's help with the matter that I was finally able to turn off the lights with no hair-raising occurrences following."

Hotel Galvez is a place of business gatherings and social events now – a wedding venue for the well-healed – and unlike other alleged haunted places, the employees of The Galvez embrace the rumors, emit pride when retelling its history, and integrate their own anecdotal experiences. The hotel even offers ghost tours and packages, as if celebrating its own whimsicality, as if whatever unearthly occurrences take place there, take place without a shred of malice and for the benefit and entertainment of others.

As Concierge Jackie Hasan put it in an ABC interview: "Our ghosts are very friendly, they really are," she said. "Some ghosts in the city are not very friendly, because they did not become ghosts through friendly means. But our ghosts here are very, very friendly."

On the Travel Channel's "Haunted Texas Hotel's Secrets," Hasan conjures up the death and destruction of the 1900 Storm, highlighting the tragic story of Sister Katherine and the orphans who perished in the Great Storm's murderous surge, adding that their corpses were discovered on the land on which Hotel Galvez was built.

Apparently ghostly happenings are pervasive throughout the hotel. Hasan, along with her trusted electromagnetic field detector and infrared thermometer, leads both the paying and non paying customers in and out of rooms, periodically checking the temperature in order to gauge whether or not a ghost is currently present. In a live episode of a local Houston station, an anchor is led on a haunted tour which begins in the lobby women's restroom, and reports on the guests who sometimes hear heavy breathing in the otherwise empty stalls.

During October the hotel offers a special "Dinner with the Ghosts" package which includes one night stay for two, the tour, a three course meal at the Galvez's restaurant, and valet parking, all for just under $200.

While the ghosts may be quantifiable, to describe Hotel Galvez is like describing fog – not how it looks but how it feels when you walk through it – actors reciting Shakespeare in an amphitheatre at night, struggling to capture what is by nature and intention intangible; the slow, romantic measure of explaining a dream. Six ivory stories topped with Spanish tile, one-of-its-kind architecture in Galveston, shaped in a boxed U, arms cradling the warm brown waters of the Gulf.

To describe Hotel Galvez is to paint summer, to smell a bride's creamy pastel bouquet of exotic flowers, to walk long carpeted halls through beams of light sculpted into patterns by the sun, interlaced and diminishing and eclipsed by long periods of darkness. To describe her is to try to escape the gaze of an ominous oil painting – the Count Viceroy Bernardo de Galvez – looming at the far end of the lobby promenade, staring at you with the quiet dispossession of a man who has never seen the island named for him but knows the secrets to it anyway.

No doubt the energy of the hotel embodies the spirit of those who loved hard, danced in broad circles, ate well, drank even better, and partied the night away, perhaps a little too much and a little too often. But without apology. At times daring, at times ecstatic, at times very sad. But always unapologetic.

This is Galveston.

The Face, in the upper center of the picture (photograph by the author)

The Face: The Haunting Truth Behind the Haunted Legend

Pareidolia, the psychological tendency for humans to find importance in otherwise insignificant events, is an unfamiliar term to most. Eighteenth Century Scottish philosopher David Hume described this fascinating phenomenon with depth and eloquence: "There is a universal tendency among mankind to conceive all beings like themselves, and to transfer to every object, those qualities, with which they are familiarly acquainted, and of which they are intimately conscious. We find human faces in the moon, armies in the clouds; and by a natural propensity, if not corrected by experience and reflection, ascribe malice or goodwill to everything, that hurts or pleases us."

Often pareidolia, pronounced *parr–i–doh–lee–a*, emerges in the religious context, and bizarrely, in food. There is the famous story of the woman in New Mexico in the late 1970s who "found" the face of Jesus in her tortilla, framed it and invited anyone interested to come to her home and witness to this Divine event. Thousands came.

In 2004 a woman sold her grilled cheese sandwich with the likeness of the Virgin Mary on Ebay for $28,000. The fact that the sandwich was ten years old and had a bite taken out of it apparently did nothing to diminish its blessed stack of carbohydrates and dairy.

Though pareidolia, from ancient Greek words which roughly translate into "wrong image" tends to slant on the religious side. This event, as noted astronomer and scientific pioneer Carl Sagan called an "evolutionary trait," also finds meaning in the world of the paranormal.

Ghost hunters see orbs of light in photographs as evidence of a ghost's appearance, and will often discover aspects to their images – human aspects – which to them can only be explained as possessing the tangible, physical manifestation of a ghost. Electronic Voice Phenomena, or EVP, the recorded sounds of the paranormal, is also called auditory pareidolia.

There are countless examples of pareidolia. On the Island, there is The Face. The story of The Face is something one hears as a kid around the bonfire, in a car driving around the Island late night as a teenager, a story told in quiet shadows in low voices, more of a rite of passage than urban legend, with the reach and force of a Category 5 hurricane.

Don't touch The Face or something bad will happen to you. The Face is the face of a demon. A young nurse once dared to touch The Face and subsequently died as she accidentally backed her car off the dock and into the water.

The Face is possibly known to a broader range of people than the mayor. Comfortably landscaped on the water side of a University of Texas Medical Branch (UTMB) building, The Face has earned its legend for several reasons. For one thing, despite repeated attempts to remove it, the striking design of shadow and rock reemerged. Twice.

The vertical rectangles of concrete directly above The Face *on two floors* have been sandblasted, appearing smooth and therefore distinct. On the first floor, just above a side door leading into the building is the unmistakable likeness of a man's face, appearing long and gaunt and a bit perturbed – or perhaps disturbed – and so the story unfolds: the inevitable (and demonic?) spirit causing The Face to exist, also causes it to relocate. The folks at UTMB reputably stopped their sandblasting party out of frustration, or as some people claim "fearing the next reemergence could only be inside the building, and nobody wants that."

And everyone hears the same story, with remarkably little to no variance: the ornery old man who owned the land prior to UTMB ordered his children never to sell the land after his death, which they most promptly did. Now the old man has cursed the building with his own likeness and evil bidding, and if one even looks for more than a minute at him, the brazen onlooker will soon meet his tragic end.

Setting aside the obvious implausibility of this legendary tale, there is no denying the facts: UTMB did repeatedly try to sandblast *something* off of the side of their building. A menacing barbed wire fence surrounds the property with the mean grimace of a prison gate, adorned with *trespassers will be prosecuted* signs like Christmas ornaments. What looks like a painfully ordinary office building – bland and unappealing – attracts enough attention to make it a Fort-Knox-meets-Alcatraz kind of forbidden.

But what exactly are they hiding, and why?

As it turns out, answering that question is as easy as writing hieroglyphics in cursive, upside down. Researching the truth behind the legend of The Face is like asking questions at a Mafia funeral: information floats around the room with the bouncing frequency of bubbles, yet everyone's words are completely empty of substance.

Who was the original of the property? From whom did UTMB purchase the property? Who is this man behind The Face? Questions – with seemingly straightforward answers – fall instead like feathers in a black hole – obliterated without even a fighting chance.

But then there's Stewart Title.

Only due to the gracious folks working at the magnum of a title insurance company and their due diligence, did the truth finally emerge.

To start at the beginning, Galveston's founding father Michel B. Menard owned the property (as he did most of the island) in the 19th Century. But according to title and deed documents dug up by Stewart Title, the Galveston Yacht Basin, Inc., along with Joe Grasso and Sons, Inc. owned the property along the harbor until the Board of Regents of the University of Texas System purchased it in early 1973.

The UTMB Geophysics Laboratory of the Marine Science Institute at Galveston, named the Maurice Ewing Hall, is just that – a hall – designated for purposes by UTMB, looking forlorn and isolated as the brown pelicans surrounding it, lacking a welcoming presence: an office building.

Or is it?

If The Face must be traced back to a man, and the mythological man behind the original story did not actually exist, why not the man for whom the building was named – a person with impressive notoriety, whose passion and commitment for his work earned him a reputation – an infamous (some might say) reputation – and whose name is a permanent title in big bold letters on the side of a building?

Maurice Ewing. Ewing was a brilliant geophysicist with a list of medals and honors as long as the Seawall – among them the 1973 National Medal of Science. Ewing died just one year after the property was purchased by UTMB. "Doc," as he was known, was named the head of the Division of Earth and Planetary Sciences of the Marine Biomedical Institute by the University of Texas in 1972.

Maurice Ewing (courtesy the Royal Melbourne Hospital)

Phrases like "driving force," "singularly responsible," and "living legacy" frequent articles describing the man. Ewing was also quite known for his intensity and lack of patience:

...a brilliant, entrepreneurial, relentlessly driven young professor named William Maurice Ewing came to Columbia with little patience for traditional geologists. "Annoying fellows," he called them, "who spend their time poking around trying to explain this or that little detail. I keep wanting to say, 'Why don't you try to see what's making it all happen?'

As a professor and department head for one of the country's largest hospital systems, it was Ewing's job to train

85

students and geophysicist hopefuls. "Ewing immersed himself and his colleagues in unprecedented explorations of the intimidating oceans," from a Columbia University biography.

Certainly being landlocked must have proved frustrating. "It's my view that we won't know where the most interesting places are until we've seen all of them," Ewing said. Ewing was studying an entity without feature on a map and yet took up 70% of it. He held the conviction that studying the ocean floor must be done by boat during a time when the belief that whatever was worth studying about the ocean floor – if anything – could be done from land. Geophysics simply did not exist at the time Ewing came on the scene. He fought for funding on projects throughout his career.

In his private life, Ewing's extremism cost him two marriages. His round-the-clock emersion – the same level of dedication which led to so many pioneering discoveries – unfolded in his persona as a series of neverending demands. Such a presence must have seemed overwhelming at times; surely his work ethic was to others a challenge. Even if his unique personality "quirks" were essential for the work he was doing.

Maurice Ewing on the left (courtesy the Royal Melbourne Hospital), and
The Face on the right (photographed by the author)

So is it Maurice Ewing – that frontiersman of the ocean – appearing on the side of building named for him? Is he angry about something – the projects gone undone for lack of funding, his work not continued in the manner he desired, demonstrating the pointlessness of studying the ocean floor from land by staring threateningly at it, or is he – even in death – refusing to back down from his work, still "trying to figure out what makes it all happen," and to that end remaining like a fixture, literally *set in stone*?

Or is that pane of concrete on the side of the UTMB building an example of how our sophisticated brain circuitry can play clever tricks on us, that the design of shadow and discoloration is coincidental, a pareidolic reflection of what our brains want us to see? And if so, what does this say about us, as humans, what are we "transferring" as Hume put it, from our own psyche?

Perhaps this is yet another question without an easy answer.

Why the Dickens is the Strand so Haunted, Anyway?

Multi-colored halos of light emerge from the shadows in neon flashes as Vicente Perez leans against a gaslit lamppost, blowing thoughtful rings of smoke into the air. As a jazz pianist and server at upscale Italian restaurant Luigi's on the Strand, Perez speaks in amiable quick bursts, his Spanish accent making his words sound more like suggestive salsa moves than speech; two points are made immediately clear. First, finding ways to engage others with the art of conversation is as inevitable an act to this man as balancing plates of food, and second, Luigi's restaurant serves up more than just scrumptious servings of rigatoni and antipasta.

"You have no idea how haunted this place is," Perez affirms in between puffs of smoke. "You see that office

89

window up there on the second floor? Two weeks ago the owner's wife was doing paperwork when all of the sudden doors began slamming open and shut for no reason. She was horrified. A server went up there to see, and before he even stepped foot onto the floor he ran back down the stairs. Oh, yeah. This building is haunted. Just ask Luigi."

To someone unfamiliar to such ethereal stories, such a tale might seem nothing more than a hyperbolic anecdote, but to Islanders, such a story is more indicative of day-to-day inevitability than it is horror fiction. Islanders live and breathe air infused with memory – an unconscious, even microcosmic remembrance of land-sweeping travesties. But it is this fact of living and breathing amongst what is left which defines Islanders now; all may be lost but most certainly not forgotten.

* * * * *

As Galveston's temperature drops, another festive year of Dickens on the Strand surrounds the distance in decorative displays of lights boxing in the Strand's ever increasing bar scene. Here on the Strand where out-of-towners walk in moneyed bunches, there seems a natural gravitation, as if the old Victorian structures were built for novelty, the streets from 20th to 25th paved so that hundreds of thousands of bikers could show off their metallic monsters, the balconies extended further so that airborne beads might glisten along their descent down their Mardi Gras celebration, and sound to echo long and narrow while parades of people smile broadly in their Victorian costumes during Dickens on the Strand.

Historically the Strand was anything but frivolous. When Galveston was incorporated in 1839, its harbor became the entryway for ships from all over the world. Since private banks had not yet been approved by Congress, financial transactions were run by private businesses – mercantile firms. The Strand's wholesalers, including cotton agents, grocery, hardware and dry goods stores, and insurance companies were bustling entities.

The Strand (which means "beach" in German, named by a German immigrant who thought "Avenue B" didn't sound elegant enough for his downtown jewelry business) was called the "Wall Street of the Southwest" for its admirable display of economic agility.

A Parade at the Strand in Olden Days (Courtesy of Rosenberg Library)

Galveston, the 4th largest city in Texas, was a booming town with a bright future.

From the *Galveston Architecture Guidebook*, by Ellen Beasley and Stephen Fox: "Here [on the Strand] is found the largest concentration of singularly important buildings in the city, as well as one of the most significant assemblages of late-19th-century commercial buildings in the country."

In the country.

Then the End of Times – a storm which would ultimately decimate the Island's economic hot air balloon, forever lending ownership to the city the title "the worst natural disaster in American history."

The morning of the Great Storm the weather was suspiciously quiet and cloud-free, but by the afternoon seventeen feet of water climbed the buildings on the Strand in menacing waves, the dank black-as-night abyss already threaded with the lifeless weightlessness of thousands of bodies – the rich, the poor, the master, the servant, the debutante, the degenerate, all floating together along with their broken homes, making history even as their bodies began to decay.

And while The Great Storm might be the most notorious of the natural disasters to pillage the Island, the tragedy was far from being the only natural disaster to go on a murderous rampage. Multiple fires ravaged the town. Yellow fever was unto itself a grand grim reaper – but that's not all. There were several wars to severely impact the Island – the bloody Battle of Galveston, and of course the hostile Civil War, reenacted on the Strand every year.

According to resident ghost expert and owner of Ghost Tours of Galveston, Dash Beardsley, the nature of how a person passes is what impacts the nature of what happens after he dies.

With so much unexpected and untimely deaths concentrated in such a relatively small area, it becomes much easier to loosen the grip on life perception and further along the intertube which is a person's willing suspension of disbelief. Whether one believes it or not, Galveston – in particular the Strand – is one of the most haunted places in the United States.

It is that famous storm, so well documented, which holds a particularly firm grip on the imagination of the masses. Along with the survivors' journals archived at the Rosenberg Library, there is research, newspaper articles, books and even a movie.

The Strand was to 1900 Galveston as Ground Zero is to the twin towers. From Ground Zero, the stories emerge.

A Photo of Luigi's From the Past (Courtesy of Rosenberg Library)

"The woman haunting the second and third floor of Luigi's was a schoolmarm," said Dash Beardsley, "she was either a teacher or a nurse, and she began pulling in bodies as they rose up out of the water. Some were dead, some were not, but she assembled them there in that building where she attended to them until her own death three months later. Many people have heard the sound of a whimpering woman coming from the second floor."

That a spirit more than a hundred years old was only recently making her sorrowful energy known speaks to the power of that energy, and the degree of the tragedy which caused it. Surely in those last months of her life remains a secret too uncomfortable and unsettling to then in afterlife become something suddenly stable. She must have winced as the wagons of bodies passed by, covered her mouth with cloth

93

as the putrid smell or burning flesh wafted down the street. This, the unforgettable aftermath of true devastation, is itself a haunting.

It is the Strand's buildings, unbothered by the frailty of life or the immeasurable force of nature, which forever look onto the street, their windows like darkened holes, punctuated and possessed, withholding from, but also tempting, the rest of the living world.

The Luigi building – like other marvels in Galveston – represent the Golden Era of Galveston, its pink and gray granite swirling in ostentatious bulges, an historic landmark and trademark of the great Galveston architect Nicholas Clayton. Galveston's founding fathers George Ball, John Hutchings, and John Sealy ran their banking and wholesale dry goods business from the building until the Civil War. Their business was the first of its kind in Texas, and from which other businesses would model themselves.

Luigi's is only one possessed establishment on the Strand. Ask the manager at the Voodoo Lounge or the folks working at Colonel Bubbies, or the desk clerks at the Tremont, or the female waitresses at the Mediterranean Cafe. What a triumphant irony of life and testimony for the resilience of Islanders that such a celebratory event such as Dickens on the Strand should be located where so many lives were lost, a place in which darkness means karaoke and bar-hopping as much as it means danger, that slow-moving, subtle lurking eye of five cobbled-stoned blocks, lit only by the hypnotic dance of small flickering fires and Christmas lights.

The Menard Mansion

The Menard Mansion:
Parties, Pow-wows, &
the Preternatural at
Galveston's Oldest Surviving Home

They're just oaks. Twisted things, knotted and gnarled, zigzagging in the sharp edged shape of lightning. Oaks. Dark undersides, draped with moss a supernatural green, jutting out from its thick trunk like fat fingers on a mutated hand, a common sight in many southern places, but not here, only a few blocks from the Gulf of Mexico.

Inside blinds raise – this happens without hands it seems – and open goes the window by the same invisible force within.

A little girl emerges wearing a brightly colored dress, as if popped from a gumball machine, giggling as she extends her tiny arms over the balcony in a display of innocuous bravado.

Then, a bride. An entourage of well-coiffed people walk by slowly, huddled together but gradually spreading out like an amoeba, laughter and smiles. This is not the wedding day but some sort of rehearsal for it, not a furrowed brow or saturated hand among them. Following the path under the great oaks the wedding party disappears into the backyard, to the gazebo, where flowers the colors of raspberries drape white wicker.

The Menard House. It is dusk and already a withdrawal of life. A gloom, dappled by crooked branches, thick and criss-crossed in layers so that not much sky shows at all – then yellows orbs of light electrify the ascending shadows, like spotlights on a stage – a house – cylindrical white pillars in the style of the Greeks – though the whole thing seems more like a grand southern plantation.

Oak trees and ionic columns have no place on an island.

But Colonel Michel Branamour Meynard wouldn't do without them. A French Canadian, Menard emigrated the trees himself. Menard, a former fur trader, Indian chief and friend to the Shawnee, saved thousands from massacre from the rival Mexican Army during the Texas Revolution, then successfully quelled their anxieties when the Mexican Army attempted to turn the Indians against the Texans. Later Menard would be among the first to sign the Texas Declaration of Independence.

For his efforts Menard was rewarded by the first Texas Congress with a "league of land." Menard chose "Lot 37" on an unincorporated marsh, a mosquito-infested plot of wilderness overrun by supposed cannibalistic people called the Karankawa. Menard chose the island along the Gulf of Mexico, a part of the country at that time considered harsh, dangerous, and generally uninhabitable; it might as well have been the moon.

Menard's story and the story of his beloved house he nicknamed "The Oaks" is the story of Galveston. What land was not given to him by the State of Texas he bought for $50,000, so that for a time he did in fact own most of the island. On his private ten acres prefabricated pine from Maine and George arrived by sailboat, the joints of the house mortised together with white lead – a structural bit of genius which kept the house from splitting at the seams during the Great Storm of 1900.

Ladies in Front of Menard House in Bygone Days
(Courtesy of Rosenberg Library)

Menard's friends the Shawnee held an annual celebration on his lawn, leaving hundreds of arrowheads in their wake. Menard spent hours conversing with them – outdoor meetings only. Menard spoke their language as fluently as he did English, both languages learned or self-taught during his days of travel and trade as he followed the Canadian line down south. The time he spent with the Indians proved fortuitous;

without the ability to communicate and desire to befriend the native tribes, along with his skills at bartering and democracy, he would not have received the title Indian Commissioner, a position ultimately leading to the state's offer of land. In this way, Menard's relationship with Native Americans plays a critical role in the establishment of Galveston.

Colonel Michel Branamour Meynard (Courtesy of Rosenberg Library)

The Menards were known for their hospitality; a May fete was held for Menard's adopted daughters, little girls dressed in one of the four seasons circling the lawn in a mobile of pastels, skipping and giggling, either unaware or unbothered by the arrowheads scuffing the bottoms of their shoes.

100

An exhibit inside the house tells its history of ballyhoo: the site of the original Mardi Gras Ball, the Menard, a party too great to be contained. When the horses and masks hit the street that raucous night in 1871, a light (or more appropriately a torch) was lit in the hearts and minds of America. *Laissez le bon temps rouler* was born.

But then, like every great story – like the story of Galveston – the torch was extinguished.

"It did cross my mind that perhaps this is a dangerous place to live," remarked Fred Burns who bought and successfully renovated the house in the early 1990s. "I'm glad my name is not Menard."

Michel Menard was married four times. Two of his wives (along with a son) met their untimely deaths inside the house, as did Menard himself of blood poisoning in 1856.

And then there was Clara. "Clara was Menard's niece. There is a legend that on her wedding night as she was about to descend the front steps to the carriage awaiting her – a carriage possibly driven by Sam Houston – she tripped and fell down the steps and broke her neck. There is said to be a breeze blowing down the steps at midnight." Burns extensively researched the property before purchasing it. His story was published in 1994 by the *Houston Chronicle*.

There is another story of an unnamed woman who broke her neck and subsequently haunts the home every Mardi Gras at midnight, appearing at the top of the steps where she fell. This story has been passed on by the men who initially worked for Menard as slaves, referring to the apparition as a "beautiful young lady."

The Menard saw the deaths of many strangers as well. The good times stopped rolling temporarily during the Civil War when the house was used as a hospital for soldiers suffering from Yellow Fever. It is difficult to imagine the picturesque Menard referred to as the "Yellow Fever Hospital."

101

Edward Ketchum was police chief during the Great Storm of 1900, when the Menard was owned by the Ketchum family. The house took in 4½ feet of water and many animals, including a cow. Ten bodies were discovered in the backyard.

Inside the Menard is every bit a living museum. Each room is staged meticulously in the Regency style of the late 19th Century, a style influenced by the Greeks, Romans, and Chinese, reflecting Menard's taste for things exotic and lively, and perhaps the man himself. The United States Department of Interior called the Menard "...one of the best examples of southern architecture." The house is listed in the Federal Archives as a National Shrine.

It seems fitting somehow that the founding father of Galveston – the man who made an entire part of the country accessible, acceptable to the rest of the world – would be as festive as he was fierce. Despite the tragedies. Despite the deaths.

The mystery of Menard is the mystique of Galveston.

The oaks are the symbol. They remain impassive in the wind. Bent at the joints as if cradling some great void. Oaks are supposed to whisper, but here at the Menard there is silence. The stillness is like a pregnant pause, glowing and alive with the density of the unknown. Did Menard build the house or was it the Allen Brothers, the founders of Houston? How did his third wife die in the house when she was just 33? Did his niece Clara really fall down the steps on her wedding day and break her neck? How did Menard himself die? History conflicts – was it blood poisoning? A back tumor? Carbuncle?

And finally, is the famous Menard – a living museum, now a place for private events and public tours cursed – haunted by the spirits whose end was met there?

Despite all the unanswered questions, he is alive here – Menard – sipping Mint Juleps on the porch – a gaze languid – an occasional creak from the wood slants beneath giving to the weight of his rocking chair. With his eyes he follows the line of breathless void to be filled in someday by the muscular arms of a live oak, standing like a sentinel over his land. Over his island. He ponders the future of the city born of his own delicious imagination.

Behind him a bride is married, a little girl laughs, a window is opened.

The Oleander Hotel, Now the Antique Warehouse

Madame Kitty and Her Haunted Oleander: Galveston's Free State Years

A shivering crowd gathers outside the New York Stock Exchange. A late October chill runs through the street, biting exposed faces and hands with the poisonous glee of an electric eel. It is 1929. Rumors of the crash were true; the crowd dries and thickens like flour, rounding the glossy downtown building in the concentric circles of electron orbitals. The greatest depression the world had ever seen.

In Galveston a crowd gathers too, the building not a skyscraper but a two story house shifting between feet – rather than solemn faces, the crowd is male and happily intoxicated, bent over and heaving, as a woman wearing a bustier the color of blood yanks two of them through the front door, her skin glowing amber by the kaleidoscopic light of the Harvest Moon.

While the rest of the world fainted into piles of collateral damage by the shotgun collapse of the American stock market, the city of Galveston blossomed out of the ground which sought to drown it. Since the devastation of the 1900 Storm, Galveston's heart began to throb again inside the money-clip grip of the tourism industry, largely spurred by the creation of the Seawall, the trendy bathhouses lining it, and the opening of the glamorous Galvez Hotel in 1911.

And thanks to the 18th Amendment ratified in 1919 prohibiting the sale of alcohol, bootlegging rumrunners openly defying the waters of the Gulf helped the Island stand upright (or perhaps more of an unstable slant). Economic security is impressive considering this was the Depression Era; women and children across the filling of the American cookie were giving up everything for a fighting chance at a slice of bread.

Ollie Quinn, the brazen leader of the Beach Gang (opposed to the Downtown Gang), buddied up to the Sicilian family who had immigrated a decade prior called the Maceos, and the first wildly successful speakeasy was born. The Hollywood Dinner Club was another Galveston-led first for the country; the closest thing to it today might be an upscale casino, if the casino had a dance floor the size of Texas, was the first of its kind to use air conditioning, and was located on an island.

The appearance of the Maceos on the stage of Galveston was timely; when the Houston Ship Channel opened in 1915, Galveston's stint among the most active ports in the country faded like a steamship in the gray midmorning fog.

Downtown Galveston another wildly successful but curiously legal business was underway. According to a former police reporter who wrote his master's thesis called "A Sociological Study of a Segregated District," Galveston had

106

more prostitutes in 1929 than Shanghai. The Red-Light District ran from Avenue A to Broadway. In just a handful of city blocks more than 50 brothels thrived, catering to military men like fast food joints; cheap and eager to satiate, with enough variety among them to ensure their clientele's regular return.

Sketch of a Turn-of-the-Century Red Light District

On the corner of Post Office and 25th, now on the outskirts of commercial downtown Galveston, stands the haunted remains of what was once a "hotbed" of activity – an African American brothel known as the Oleander Hotel. When the building was discovered after years of neglect, the trappings of a bordello emerged like fossils from extinction, single light bulbs dangling from the ceiling with the minimalist melodrama of a torture chamber, disembodied broomsticks leaning against the wall, faltering on their clothes-hanging duties.

The Antique Warehouse is its own fossil-bed of trinkets, oversized mirrors, peeling furniture, and just about anything one could imagine – a true warehouse – but upstairs is more like a museum.

Corner View of the Antique Warehouse – the old Oleander

The Oleander Hotel. Think Black Dahlia. Black Dahlia was the nickname given to a wannabe young ingénue in the 1920s brutally murdered in Los Angeles. Elizabeth Short, with her jet black hair and ice blue eyes enraptured the country. The media dowsed themselves in her story and drowned everyone else. Books, movies, and many speculations later, the mystery revolving around Elizabeth Short's murder remains, despite a reported *50 people* "confessing" to the infamous homicide.

Like the intriguing soft darkness of Black Dahlia, mystery snakes around what was once a glass box of wild vines – an atrium – with the romance of a hushed silence. There is something slightly sinister about the second floor of the Antique Warehouse, something so delicately feminine, one might think a sound might break it.

Rooms. Impossibly small rooms line the interior would-be atrium like Lego blocks, doors flung open, their splintered wood invitations to a world now shrouded in dust. These are exhibits, these rooms – museum exhibits – but rather than Sacajawea and saber toothed tigers, live reminders of a boudoir history, beds, lacey clothes, things for sale. Always, things for sale.

The famous round bed of Madam Kitty

At the start of the tour, Madame Kitty's boudoir, a bed the size and color of a fully ripened rose, like the Madame herself – a painting – dark ringlets positioned perfectly, loose enough so that they might straighten, her voluptuous body more an exclamation than a point. The framed License for Prostitution certificate resting atop a desk signed by the Madame emerges like a movie prop; but the truth is never so styled.

Imagine a summer in the south without air conditioning, an occasional breath of air fluting in from the atrium the only sign of the outside world. One single light bulb dangles from the ceiling with the ego of a spotlight, illuminating with punctuation a central spot, darkening beyond pain the rest. The door, with its newest lock bangs shut, stuffing in the heat with the presumption of a greenhouse. And then the single light is extinguished and you are left with a stranger, a man who has not yet bathed from his long day unloading fish on the dock. When he exits there is just you and a wall of suffocating blackness.

Madame Kitty

The Oleander was a fully functioning brothel and Madame Kitty one of the savviest businesswomen of her time, but the place was packed, as unclean and cluttered as a bus station in downtown Calcutta.

110

The folks – Scott and Holly Hansen – who bought the place appreciated its history and so sought to keep the rooms as they were; amounts scribbled in no discernible order – monetary sums the women were due perhaps – penciled lines still visible on the walls, numbers like symbols from the brothel days when hope meant adding up.

This is a cobwebbed existence, a thinly veiled veneer, an energy more live than dead; it's palpable, more obviously haunted than perhaps any of Galveston's spiritual graves. A brothel for the paranormal.

Owner Scott Hansen talks about the day a most intriguing man walked into their shop: "He was big and grizzly, with lots of white hair. He found me and asked if I wanted to know the history of my building. I said I did." Hansen looks up at nothing and pauses. The pause lasts. He stands in a closet-sized room, talking rushed between breaths as if expecting to be interrupted. "The man said he was an orphan here, and that he used to go to sleep to the music of a blind piano player named Blind Willie. Madame Kitty took pity on him as an orphan."

Clyde Wood of The Witchery organized his Galveston Ghost Hunters, a "paranormal meet-up group" to gather at the Antique Warehouse after hours one night:

When the time was up for the last group I started rounding everyone up. The upstairs is huge and it took a while to locate everyone. The last person was one of our more "sensitive" members and when I came upon her in one of the small rooms she said she couldn't leave! She was frozen in place! I asked her what was wrong and she said a little girl had her by the hand and wouldn't let her go! She was visibly upset, so I talked her through a visualization until she was released.

There was one spot in particular the group collectively agreed had stopped them right in their tracks. "Right over here," Hansen says, walking toward the far corner of the first hallway. Unlatching the mesh door, he walks into a blind spot,

111

a dark pocket of space closed off from the public, with a pleasant draft of cool air swirling down from the high windows.

"This here was the kitchen, and possibly where the women were examined by doctors." Another long pause, and then he seems to drift. Words he can't bring himself to say from a reality he can't imagine.

"Might be why folks talk about this spot so much." He begins walking toward the mesh door again and turns to look. He is now lost in shadows. A buzz saw and a car's radio in the far off distance. A snap back into the moment, and the shadows recede. "Just yesterday a family asked me if this place was haunted and when I said yes, they said they knew it. Because of this." Hansen stops talking as suddenly as he began, as though asked a question, when there is nothing. But it's soft, this nothing.

"Myself I've only had a couple experiences, but they were both really powerful. Once I came up here to get something and for no reason at all the hair stood straight up on the back of my neck. Let me tell you I couldn't get back down to the first floor fast enough. I was spooked."

Hansen is called from downstairs. "This here was for the clients," and points upward toward a door above the stairs marked *Gentlemen.*

Some haunted places – like the Galvez and the Tremont – are so well groomed it is difficult to imagine anything beyond what a high-priced vacuum and chemical won't cover up. But here, at the Oleander, the awareness is more like a carnival playhouse – with every sense you are involved. You intake the dusty breath of things born of another century, your shape seems to twist and distort. You are chilled to the bone.

Up on the second floor is pink and red and silk, is communicative wood floors and blurry daylight, old things – books and lamps and paintings and chairs – the handsome sacred keepsakes of grandmother's attic. Up here is Galveston's Red Light District, a time when the Island was financially sound compared to the rest of the world. Up here is Black Dahlia, the gravest of sins and the most exquisite of sinners, a combination of beauty and depravity so painful and utterly captivating you cannot help but confess.

The Samuel May Williams House: The Haunting Impact of Galveston's Peculiar Institution

His posture seemed impossibly erect – stiffened by discomfort – as if standing against an invisible rock wall. He stepped onto the balcony of Ashton Villa with a slow and steady focus, his wide forehead like white space on the page of a magazine, bringing great attention to the severity of his gaze. Then the general said what he had come to say:

The people of Texas are informed that, in accordance with a proclamation from the Executive of the United States, all slaves are free. This involves an absolute equality of personal

115

rights and rights of property between former masters and slaves, and the connection heretofore existing between them becomes that between employer and hired labor. The freedmen are advised to remain quietly at their present homes and work for wages. They are informed that they will not be allowed to collect at military posts and that they will not be supported in idleness either there or elsewhere.

Highly decorated General Gordon Granger, along with 1800 Union soldiers, travelled to the Island to enforce the Emancipation Proclamation ordered by President Lincoln three years prior, a decree all but ignored in the South. It was a sweltering summer – that June of 1865- but no one would remember the heat.

Before he could withdraw within the Villa the crowd floundered, shaken. Men and women, worn and weary, threw up their hands and touched the ground, a moment too precious to let float, untethered. A young mother, formerly bound by a promise she did not herself give, grabbed her child in a bewildered act of protection. There was an element of chaos in this.

The following year the annual celebration began. Juneteenth, yet another Galveston-led first.

Twenty years prior.

It was mid-morning and Sarah attended to her vegetable garden, picking peas and mulling over the bad asparagus. *Why were they withering?* Over the pasture, in the slave quarters, the smell of baking bread wafted like a temptress through the chimney into the free air, as Sarah's four children attended to their studies in the schoolhouse their magnanimous father had built for them.

Founder of Texas Navy Samuel May Williams, the brilliant entrepreneur and banker, a man who possessed the foresight and financial ambition to add a cupola atop his home so he could keep his savvy eye on incoming ships (and then

116

rush downtown and engage in commodities trading) was away on business. Sam's absence was nothing new; during his and Sarah's marriage, he had been away a vast majority of the time. Being Governor Stephen F. Austin's Secretary of State and general right-hand man held as much prestige as it did demand.

Samuel May Williams (Courtesy of Rosenberg Library)

The air dropped dew into the early evening air as an oversized pot roast rested like a steaming centerpiece on the Williams' dinner table. Inside the slave quarters a quiet hush

117

fell over the family of three, each moving in concentric overlapping circles, with the measured movements of a tightly choreographed dance. In their eyes an expression lingered like an echo. Within them seethed the sunken something of withdrawal.

The hush unraveled like a coil when she left – the matriarch – the moment she walked out of the kitchen and into the main house. Heat from the oven bent over the bricks like a slap. Outside the shrill wheeze of frogs sounded manic.

Their dance, along with the wheezing of the frogs, halted to a point of breathlessness. Then they waited. Yelling from within the main house – the Williams house – violence in the cadence and volume – they could hear her sobbing in sheer desperation and pleas, but the damage had clearly been done. And discovered.

* * * * *

The Samuel May Williams home is one of the most important homes in Galveston – the Island's second oldest and for a time a museum – faces sideways from the street like a dismissal. The legend of its haunting is one of the Island's lesser known, and Samuel May Williams only mentioned with the occasional nod in Texas history. After Sam's wife had begun choking that night, crushed glass was found in her food, and until Sam's return the family's cook was locked underneath the house. This might have been weeks or longer.

As the story goes, Sarah's mistress haunts the restored home (now a private residence), her presence as much a part of the home's distinctiveness as the cupola from which Sam once made a fortune. When the house was a museum, guests spoke of seeing a woman standing at the top of the stairs. Others expressed feeling a "feminine presence" throughout the house.

118

The house is no longer a museum but is so well maintained it appears new – a bright white plantation-style boxy cottage with a mini red box just behind it.

Historic View of the Samuel May Williams House
(Courtesy of Rosenberg Library)

While the Samuel May Williams house is upheld – as it Samuel May Williams himself – as one of the most important historic island landmarks in Galveston, there is something lurking beneath – inside – something venomous and unearthly.

Ghosts, like humans, come in different forms. Dash Beardsley of Ghost Tours of Galveston says that people become ghosts when their death was untimely, tragic, and unexpected, as is the case with many Island hauntings.

A person may also transition into the astral plane when that person possesses much greed or banal desires within them, unfilled wishes such as revenge, when their death was violent or their life degraded. Not all spirits are created equal. The Spiritual Science Research Foundation (SSRF), a group of Indian doctors, categorizes spirits in a hierarchy based on "relative strength," with *Common Ghost* at the bottom and *Subtle Sorcerer* at the top. Based on "percent of people affected," however, demons rank first. SSRF believes 50% of people are affected by demons.

Newspaper archives from the *Houston Telegraph* and a book published in 1961 entitled *The Galveston Era: the Texas Crescent on the Eve of Secession* by Earl Wesley Fornell, paint a curiously positive picture of slave life in Galveston:

By the very nature of their station the fifteen hundred slaves living on the Galveston Island ought to have been considered the least privileged group residing in the city; yet, from many points of view, this was not the case, for the actual privileges enjoyed by a vast number of the more fortunate slaves on the Island were many indeed. The Negroes loved the Island life and were always loathe to leave it...Among the leading citizens on the Island it was considered to be a mark of gentility not only to take good care of one's Negroes, but also to allow them to indulge their love for "fancy clothes."

The Williams family was most assuredly one of Galveston's most elite. Does this mean that behind closed doors their slaves were "privileged"? Can these reports even be trusted? African Americans were not afforded the rights to education and so the authors of historical documents portraying slave life in a favorable manner were more than likely slave owners themselves. One wonders what an Island slave would have said if asked about the quality of his life.

Adding to the curious behavior of the Williams' slaves is Williams himself. In *Samuel May Williams, Early Texas Entrepreneur* by Margaret Swett Henson, the political endeavors of Williams are detailed. While dealing with the British with regard to cotton trade "...Williams wrote a lengthy memoir defending the struggle against Santa Anna and emphasizing the necessity for slave labor in cotton production."

In her book *De Leon, a Tejano Family History,* Carolina Castillo Crimm writes of Williams' business dealings in his attempts to expand his interests in Texas, including some less than popular transactions on land speculation. "When word reached Texas of the massive land sales, Williams and his partners were condemned as land speculators for planning to profit from the remaining public lands in Texas."

Crimm goes on to discuss the disintegration of Williams and Stephen F. Austin's relationship: "He [Austin] spent the remainder of his days denying any involvement and disassociating himself from his one-time friend. Samuel May Williams, perhaps the most hated man in Texas, never did gain all the land he had been promised nor make good on any of the promissory notes."

Most hated man in Texas. Samuel Williams, a leading mercantile businessman and founding father of Galveston, a controversial figure in Texas history infamous for his self-serving motivations, a supporter of the "peculiar institution" of slavery.

Galveston is haunted by more than just a few peculiarities.

In Closing

It is the Saturday night before Halloween. Galveston has been relatively quiet since the boisterous balmy days of summer, a silence of withdrawal. The moon shines silver in an otherwise dead black sky. Along the rumpled, cobblestone street known to tourists as The Strand, and to locals as simply 'downtown', celebrators flank doorways clinging to their beer, dressed in all manner of garish costume.

The band currently playing at Oktoberfest just a few blocks away makes the air pulsate staccato, and the thumping bass measures like an overactive heartbeat. Over at Saengerfest Park, six full-grown adults attempt to dance Michael Jackson's *Thriller*, their imitation red leather jackets – like their choreography – more than just a stone's throw away from the original.

Yaga's, which hasn't been even half full since school started, is now happy and alive, windows opened wide to the street, allowing patrons to enjoy the first real cold-front of the year, the frisky cool air like good news after an extended downturn of events. Down at the end of the street in front of the old railroad museum stands a group of maybe 100, huddling together in jackets and hats, facing the street as if organizing themselves for parade.

Before them professes an extraordinary looking man – tall, with long blond hair and full-length black jacket – extending his arms in dramatic flapping waves as though attempting flight. In any other place such a scene might seem bizarre, but on The Strand the Saturday night before Halloween it all makes perfect sense. Dash Beardsley enthusiastically prepares this evening's group for the most infamous haunted ghost tour on the Island.

And while the dazzle of music and lights and three-quarters moon seem so contrary to darkness – so pedestrian – the old buildings lining the streets, and their sunken leering windows couldn't be more ominous. If energy is never completely destroyed the answer to the feeling is obvious. People died by the hundreds on these streets, many times over. Bodies piled on top of another and burned. By scientific law they – their energy – lives on.

It is that ethereal something no one can quantify, that void in the most fundamental understanding of life. Unexplainable even by science. Galveston awakens from unconsciousness during these events, holidays, the summer season, but inside the gap she lingers. When the moon is full and a crowd gathers under the bright streetlights, the flickering of that unexplainable something emerges from dormancy like a zombie, or so it seems. Between you and me, the scariest part of Halloween isn't the bloody, lifelike wolf mask or the hair-raising, passionately-told ghost stories, or even the illuminated sky, but the Unknown – the roving shadows and the inky blackness pressing like an oncoming storm against a tabula rasa of windows. Windows that have born vacant witness to the grotesque realities of which the living can only emulate.

Gargoyle at Bishop's Palace

Index

CPSIA information can be obtained at www.ICGtesting.com
Printed in the USA
BVOW11s1004281015

424000BV00018B/247/P